Water Damage 1/25/11

All In My *Mind?*

Jennifer Busch

Copyright © 2010 Jennifer Busch

All rights reserved. No part of this book may be reproduced in any form without prior written permission from the publisher. The author and publisher disclaim all liability in connection with the use of this book.

This book contains the ideas and opinions of its author and is intended solely to provide helpful information. The reader should consult his or her medical, health, or other competent professional before adopting any of the suggestions in this book.

Quantity discounts are available on bulk orders. Contact sales@TAGPublishers.com for more information.

TAG Publishing, LLC
2618 S. Lipscomb
Amarillo, TX 79109
www.TAGPublishers.com
Office (806) 373-0114
Fax (806) 373-4004
info@TAGPublishers.com

ISBN: 978-1-934606-26-1
Library of Congress Control Number: 2010927862

First Edition

All In My *Mind?*

Jennifer Busch

Just because Fate doesn't deal you the right cards, it doesn't mean you should give up. It just means you have to play the cards you get to their maximum potential.

- Les Brown

Dedication

Dr. Richard E. Busch – Rick, my husband, who loved me no matter what and shared each of my first-steps. He never allowed me to give in or give up. You are my blessing.

Elaina, my oldest, who taught her younger sister many things that a mother might teach - to tie her shoes and ride a bike. Elaina always tried to please and never complained when she was let down. She possesses a sweet, gentle and Christian heart.

Olivia, my youngest, who was always willing to climb into my bed and watch The Waltons and made me feel I was still giving something back to her. Whether she knew it or not, she gave me her energy and love when I did not feel I deserved it. She too has a sweet Christian heart.

Elaine, my mom, how do I make the words "thank you" ring with the true meaning in my heart? As I write this dedication I look back at your unwavering love and marvel at your ability to stay the course. I know this road has not been easy but you gave me your strength. Though there were some scary times, you never showed your fear. I know you are my mother but you are also my best friend, and I love you. I will always be here for you, and I want to be as caring as you are for me!! I love you!

About the Author

Jennifer E. Busch went to work for *The American Chiropractor* magazine right out of high school. She worked up the ladder of the business from assistant to the publisher, to national marketing manager and finally to general manager.

Jennifer married Dr. Richard E. Busch III, in 1996 and together they founded and developed a leading chiropractic clinic that is now nationally recognized for a successful and non-surgical treatment, the DRS Protocol™, for severe disc conditions.

After the birth of her second child, Jennifer became very ill with a long–term undiagnosed condition. After searching through years of various medical and alternative treatments and therapies, eventually it was discovered that she was in the critical stage of adrenal exhaustion.

Jennifer credits her strong faith and will to survive for her success, and though there are still occasional setbacks, she is dedicated to overcoming adrenal fatigue and living the best life possible. Jennifer lives with her husband and her two children in the Fort Wayne, Indiana area.

Acknowledgements

Amanda: Thank you for being calm and nonjudgmental.

Angi: Thank you, my friend since childhood, you would drop everything to come and be with me.

Bill: I want to thank you for drilling holes in our house and tearing off trim to prove to me there was no imaginary mold and for looking for any of the other obsessive, compulsive things I imagined.

Christie: Thank you for doing all the extras above and beyond.

Dr. Denise: Thank you for a lifetime friendship and returning my calls even when you were swamped.

Donna: Thank you, Aunt Donna, for always being with me and there for me.

Eric: You are a great brother; thanks for making me laugh.

Jaclyn: Thank you, because you are always sharing and thinking of me.

Janet W: Thank you for a positive and spiritual atmosphere.

Molly: I met you in a dream, thank you for being with me and providing an unconditional love.

Rachel: Thank you my dear friend for all the diversion and never turning away, even though I may have sometimes shut you out.

Foreword

Jennifer Busch encourages others to overcome any odds that might stand in their way.

I have had the privilege to meet and get to know Jennifer and have learned much from her story of resilience in the face of adrenal fatigue syndrome.

All In My Mind? has translated Jennifer's natural warmth and empathy to a world of those who suffer as she once did. I want to thank her for instilling hope in others who are suffering from chronic conditions and showing them the path to overcome their fear. By becoming her own health advocate, Jennifer took charge of her health and found her way back to wholeness and you can too.

All In My Mind? is an inspiring read that will help sufferers navigate their feelings of frustration and vulnerability. Through step-by-step actions, Jennifer explains the reality of adrenal fatigue in the traditional medical system and offers hope to those who have been similarly frustrated by the lack of answers and empathy.

As you read through these pages you will find her journey was not easy, and often was filled with sadness, loneliness and even feelings of despair. Yet, there never came a time that she believed that her condition was all in her mind, contrary to what many doctors commonly say to adrenal fatigue patients. While you would expect that this experience might have darkened Jennifer's view of life's possibilities, instead you will find a loving, caring friend that shares with you her years of searching and ultimate triumph.

Jennifer urges anyone who is suffering from a chronic condition to trust their instincts, and as she has said many times, "If I'd been fortunate enough to have had a book like this, one that made me know about the steps of this journey and that someone else actually cares, it would have made my life make much more sense, and I would have known there was hope and even triumph."

"When there is hope in the future, that gives you power in the present."

-Les Brown

Les Brown, founder of Les Brown Enterprises, is the leading authority on releasing human potential and enhancing lives. As a renowned professional speaker, personal development and speech coach, author and former television personality, Les Brown has risen to national and international prominence by challenging individuals to live up to their greatness."

Contents

Poem: In Your Eyes	15
Chapter 1: Am I Crazy?	17
Chapter 2: My Missing Life	31
Chapter 3: Adrenal Fatigue & Related Syndromes	49
Chapter 4: Crossing the Metabolic Threshold	65
Chapter 5: The Emotion of Frustration	81
Chapter 6: The First Steps	99
Chapter 7: Is My Body the Enemy?	115
Chapter 8: Do I Have to be Special?	133
Chapter 9: Living Again	151
Adrenal Fatigue Symptom Matrix	165
Additional Resources	171
Glossary	173

In Your Eyes

How can you get so much strength in
someone's gaze?
So much laughter and memories?
So much rest?

How can you get so much joy?
So much sorrow?
So much love?
So much hate?

How can you get someone's emotion and
someone's fate?

How can I see the love in someone's eyes?
But the world in yours?

\- *Elaina Busch*

Chapter 1

Am I Crazy?

Without faith a man can do nothing; with it all things are possible.

- Sir William Osler

Young girls and boys grow up with the expectation that their lives will be wonderful, and I was no exception. I believed I would marry, have children, and accomplish something meaningful with my life. My mother always told me, "You are on Earth for a reason." Although I was unsure of what that reason would be, I have held on to her words during my darkest days.

In 1990, I was young and ready to strike out and see what life had to offer. I worked for a publishing company owned by longtime family friends. I enjoyed the business and found it to be fulfilling. I liked working and learned quickly that a strong work ethic was respected—an ideology that influenced who I would eventually become. The culture of the publishing office was extreme stress, and overachieving was the philosophy. I transformed from a fledgling, 19-year-old girl to a business woman within a remarkably short time.

During this time, I started dating the man who would ultimately become my husband. We were at different places in our lives and looking back, it was much like a merger of two companies with decidedly different ways of doing things. I was a savvy, high-energy go-getter, ready to get things done and done quickly—no excuses. Rick was a newly -graduated doctor, ready to use his skills to help and heal others. Together, we were a team committed to launching his new practice.

I enthusiastically dove into helping him build his business while continuing to work at the publishing company. At the time, I anticipated this would be the most difficult period of my life as there was so much to accomplish. I worked 70 hours per week, and yet we struggled to stay afloat financially. Still, I had no sense of the real journey that lay in wait for me, four short years down the road.

My husband, Rick, and I started our family with all the dreams and expectations many young couples experience. We welcomed our first daughter in 1997. I found motherhood to be wonderful, although it was a somewhat overwhelming experience. We had a lot of love but little money, and financial support from family was not a practical reality. We lived as many young families do, with ups and downs. Stress was ever present, both in our business and our finances, and there was emotional pain and distress as we experienced several miscarriages.

In the year 2000, our second child was born. Her birth set off a storm within my body that turned my world upside down. I was so thankful and grateful to have a healthy little girl, but for some reason those feelings of happiness and joy were quickly overshadowed. I experienced overwhelming fatigue and the unsettling feeling that I was dying.

One week after giving birth, I lay crying on our kitchen floor. I was trying to tell my husband I felt like I was dying and that something was seriously wrong. As happens with many women who experience this syndrome, these symptoms were dismissed as a postpartum hormonal swing. This explanation seemed reasonable and fit the circumstances, but I was not a first-time mother. Although I accepted this explanation, part of me knew—just knew—that something was terribly wrong. It turned out I was right.

The birth of my daughter started my long journey with adrenal fatigue syndrome. Many people who suffer from adrenal fatigue syndrome, chronic fatigue, or fibromyalgia have often experienced this same *knowing*. These diagnoses sometimes are used interchangeably, although there are some differences. However, low adrenal function is common for most sufferers of these syndromes, so they will experience many of the same emotional and physical complaints.

No matter how sincere those around you are in trying to explain to you why you feel the way you do, there is still a deep and abiding knowledge that they are wrong. You feel death breathing on the back of your neck, as surely as the sun sets. Only others who suffer from a similar condition can accurately understand this feeling and realize how it affects you. This is why it can be so difficult for those around you to offer support or to know what to do. Sadly, it is difficult for them to believe you have anything physically wrong with you at all.

When this feeling of death refused to leave me, I clung to my faith. There had to be an answer. As I revisit the feelings and emotions of those early days of my illness, I can see the plan God had in store for me. Everything I had experienced up to that moment gave me the tools that would eventually lead me down the path to a solution. Working at a publishing company gave me an education on alternative health, chiropractic care, and nutritional therapies, which opened my mind to ideas outside the traditional medical field. My mother is also a firm believer in alternative healthcare, and she supported me without question. It was as if I were being prepared by God for that higher purpose I was meant to accomplish.

After helping my husband start his practice, we worked together to serve others who were sick and suffering. This gave us both a unique perspective from which to convey our experiences. I just never imagined it would be me who would soon be the sick and suffering. God knew I could not give empathy and help others until I had experienced the magnitude of this agonizing condition for myself.

Weeks after giving birth, I had an appointment with my OB/GYN. As I sought to explain my feelings of fatigue and death, I could immediately tell he did not understand. It was as if he had already jumped to a judgment in his mind, and there I sat uselessly talking. It was as if I were explaining the blue sky to a blind person. When I finally stopped to take a breath, he immediately jumped in and announced I had a classic case of postpartum depression. He attempted to reassure me I was normal and this would pass, but I had a sinking feeling in my heart. I knew this was not a typical case of the baby blues. It was something far more devastating.

Postpartum depression is experienced by many women. It usually refers to high anxiety and heightened emotionality after childbirth caused by hormonal readjustment. This can have an impact on one's mental state, but it usually dissipates within a few weeks or months. I struggled to explain to my doctor this was something much more. My endless sense of impending death was all-consuming. I was so terribly tired. I did not have the strength to do anything more than lie on the couch. Still, he insisted his diagnosis was correct and that time would alleviate my problem.

I have been around doctors for much of my life, and I wanted to be a compliant patient and believe my doctor was probably right. My husband treats people every day, and his patients have to believe in his knowledge and skill in order to get better—so that is what I did. I believed this doctor had my best interest at heart. I did as he suggested, and I tried to resume my normal hectic life, all the while feeling as if I were running on empty.

While I had been a highly motivated, goal-orientated person, soon I was an "overachiever." It was as if everything in my life had to be perfect; I was determined to make it so, no matter how bad I felt. My grandmother had a daunting philosophy, "Keep your house in order and all other things will fall into place." I carried this advice to the extreme, reasoning that if everything around me were in a right order, then my health would follow.

I was obsessed with keeping our home clean, organized, and smelling wonderful. Daily cleaning schedules, feeding schedules for the children, and re-cleaning schedules dominated my life. I hired a cleaning lady to help, yet I would clean again the next day as if she had never been there. I found comfort in my busyness, and I clung to those routines as if my life depended on them—and in a way, it did. As long as I thought I was moving forward and controlling something, I could almost ignore what my body was trying to tell me. My mind, however, knew differently. I have no doubt this attempt to look "perfect" was merely to camouflage what was really happening to me.

Soon, my obsession with perfection spilled over to my children. I wanted my children always to be clean, pretty, and well mannered. I would insist they bathe morning and night, and sometimes after lunch if I *thought* they were too messy. I was a devoted mother, tidy housekeeper, and tried to be the best businessperson I could be. I wanted the work completed at the office, and to be performed perfectly. This created some friction because my husband was the boss, yet I was acting like a little dictator.

When you become obsessed with making everything look perfect on the outside (as I did), you soon begin to believe your own PR. When I was young, I was repeatedly told the circumstances of your life exist because you chose to allow them to exist. I also knew that I alone could choose to change those circumstances. This hypothesis added to my obsessive behavior. I reasoned that if I look good then I will feel good, and I do not want to feel bad—or do I?

One marker of adrenal fatigue syndrome is that you find yourself in an incessant state of doubt. This leads you to question your actions, your words, and even your thoughts and emotions. Because most everyone told me I was fine (after all, I *looked* fine), I blocked out the small inner voice that nagged at me and whispered otherwise. I refused to believe I was sick because that was not the person I wanted to be. My desire was to be well, happy, and perfect, but I was nothing more than a perfect shell of that person.

I had heard of and read about a type of patient categorized as "chronic." The chronic patient is one that has a condition lasting for a period of at least three months, and some may have a degree of psychological need to hold onto their illness or problems. I feared this was me and associated my problem with a great deal of negativity. I was ashamed and embarrassed by the thought this might be all in my mind because of some need for attention.

I cannot tell you the number of times I thought I was crazy. The idea that this might be true escalated my obsessions and denials to a point of an almost frenzied existence. It was as if I were afraid to step off the merry-go-round for even a second on the chance I would fall into an abyss of depression that was continually threatening to overwhelm me. Somehow, I rationalized if I ran hard enough and fast enough, it would not catch me. At some level, I also knew it would not be long before the little stamina I had left disappeared. I had to deal with the underlying issue regardless of what anyone else thought. I knew I was not crazy. I just had to prove it.

When one door of happiness
closes, another opens; but
often we look so long at the
closed door that we do not
see the one which has been
opened for us.

- Helen Keller

Chapter 2

My Missing Life

Hope never abandons you; you abandon it.

- George Weinberg

It was a distressing time for me because my life sped by in some respects and crept along in others during those trying weeks and months after my second child was born. I worked so hard to hold my life together, but little by little, cracks started to show in the "House of Perfect" I tried to build. I rushed from activity to activity trying to keep up, all the while ignoring my worsening health. It seemed as though life existed around me, but I was not emotionally participating. I felt pressure to be happy, excited, and thrilled with life. There was every reason I should have felt happy, excited and thrilled, but the best I could do was to pretend I felt those emotions.

My husband's career was making real headway. He had learned new, cutting-edge techniques to help patients with severe and chronic back problems. I was so proud of his dedication to his patients and of his ability to help the sickest patients with his calm, inner grace. I, on the other hand, could not seem to break free from the fog and doom that shrouded my mind. I was spiraling into a black hole of fatigue as my symptoms worsened.

Night intensified my feelings of helplessness. It was the only time of the day I had absolutely nothing to do but focus on my problems. Consequently, it became a very sad time for me, and I started having trouble getting to sleep. This was very difficult considering I had two young children, and I did not have the luxury of catching up on my sleep during the day. Additionally, I was still feeling the effects of a night-time feeding schedule for my youngest. I began to take anything that would help me sleep: over-the-counter sleep aids, cold medicines, anything that might make me drowsy. Sometimes it took more than one dose just to go to sleep.

The best these over-the-counter medications could do was put me into the first stage of sleep. I would routinely be awake between the hours of 2:30 a.m.- 5:00 a.m., and I felt as if I had never slept. I existed in a perpetual state of desperation. I continuously needed rest, but I was unable to get a restful, relaxing sleep. Sleeping became the major focus of each day. I mentally prepared myself before going to bed, hoping I would finally get some rest, but also wondering how long I would lie awake staring at the ceiling. The dream of being able to sleep would compel me to buy any bath salts or body creams that promoted the benefits of "relaxation" and a "restful night's sleep." Imagine going through the drug store and consistently scanning the bath aisle, hoping that "this or that" product was going to do the trick. Now this seems ridiculous, but then I was desperate.

When I would wake from a light sleep, it was as if my thoughts were speeding along, unimpeded. I would worry and fret about anything imaginable, even if it were irrational. I would worry about losing someone I loved—my mother or my children, perhaps. I worried they might get a terminal illness or have an accident. As remote as those possibilities were, I lived these scenarios in my mind as if they were real. I would wake my husband while crying inconsolably.

I now understand these episodes were panic attacks, which are symptomatic of adrenal fatigue. Most mornings I would feel a brief respite, but as the day progressed, I would work myself into an inevitable panic attack.

Further complicating my problems were the horrible night sweats. I would awaken with my skin covered in a layer of cold, slimy sweat. How could I be freezing and sweating at the same time? This would continue to the point of having to change into dry pajamas. I had a terrible time staying warm, and I would sleep with as many as three blankets piled on me while wearing both my pajamas and a bathrobe. I resorted to sleeping with a heating pad, and wearing full length flannel pajamas and a robe to bed along with my usual blankets.

I did not understand how I could be so cold yet sweat profusely during the night. This continued for months, and my days dragged on as if I were doing time in a prison cell. I was in a prison, but the prison was my own body. I physically felt as if I were going through shock, because I would be freezing all day. It was unbearable. I would bathe in scalding water, two or three times a day, just to elevate my body temperature and that was my only relief. After my bath, I would put on layers of warm underwear, pajamas, my husband's heavy robe, and thick, thick socks. One hot July day, I even built a fire in our fireplace to warm up the house. Try explaining that to the neighbors! Still nothing worked, and I was miserable.

Many mornings I would drag myself out of bed and immediately feel aching, muscle pain. It was as if someone had beaten me with a rolling pin during the night. If anyone touched my arm or even grazed my forearm, I would feel as if I had been bruised. The pain and achiness overwhelmed my entire body; I felt as if I had the flu. When I was warm, I was too warm. In fact, I felt *hot*. I would take my temperature and expect the thermometer to read 104 degrees, but it would only register 99 degrees! It was like fire and ice in the same body, and there was no middle ground. I was ice cold or burning hot and could find no comfort level at all. I was disappointed and confused. I wanted substantiation that I was not crazy!

The body is incredibly complex. It can make you feel particular symptoms, yet it may never give you solid proof of a problem. Therein, lies one of the most frustrating aspects of this illness. Many doctors approach healthcare with, almost exclusively, a scientific mindset—one that requires testing and documentation to back up the symptoms you report. Even though I knew how I felt, it was devastating not to be able to find any proof or to understand what was happening. I could never retrieve enough information from a doctor to calm my own doubts and prove that this was real.

The reality of adrenal fatigue is you may rarely, if ever, have the hard scientific data required for a diagnosis. This is because many of the symptoms are also symptomatic of other issues, and if the doctor truly believes that the problem is an emotional one, you will not get the tests you need. You must believe in your instincts and never blindly follow the medical mindset that maintains, "If you cannot scientifically show me data, then it must be a psychological problem." This position allows doctors to convince patients to accept antidepressants, counseling, or some other treatment panacea, and none of these will ever address the real cause of the problem. Had I not been determined to set aside the medical profession's convictions, I might never have escaped the prison of fatigue and my own feelings of doubt and inadequacies.

When you are forced to navigate this medical minefield, searching for proof causes additional stress. For those suffering from adrenal fatigue, any stress is bad stress. There were several stressful instances in my life that escalated my health problems and accelerated my condition. Although the stressful incidents were horrific to endure, they may have spared me from many more years of suffering as the intensifying of my symptoms is what drove me to seek a solution.

My first major stress challenge involved someone who was close to us. This person was in financial trouble and needed major assistance. Problems of any kind can be exacerbated by financial strife, and this was no exception. My husband felt obligated to give what little we had. While I was raised to believe that friends and family are very important, and I admired my husband's open heart, a part of me resented that he was giving away what we needed. We, too, had obligations and a business to run. My resentment soon showed itself through my actions and words while the stress compounded my fatigue.

The pressure from this overwhelming financial burden was enough to emotionally bury me. My husband is, and was, able to perform under high levels of emotional stress, but I suppressed everything and focused on moving forward. This suppressed, false existence became my way of life, so much so that over time the only way I felt normal was when I was in a stressed and highly anxious mode. My body was constantly churning and revved up like a high powered machine. I always had a sensation of a low vibration or noise within me as if my motor had to be running at all times.

Each day, after emotionally pushing myself through work, during the drive home the fatigue slammed into my body, and once I finally arrived home I dragged myself through the door. A deep, internal shakiness accompanied my stress and fatigue. Mere words cannot possibly explain what this was like. The stress and fatigue were relentless. I often said, "It's as if someone is pumping poison through my veins." It was a feeling of absolute, slow death!

The body's response to stress is called "fight or flight." It produces adrenaline that comes from the adrenal glands perched atop each kidney like a small cap. When you are faced with fear and danger, your adrenal glands release a flood of adrenaline that is instant energy and triggers many sympathetic systems which include the brain and muscle responses allowing you to fight off the danger and flee to safety. In ancient times, the "flight" reaction was highly advantageous; it would be imperative to escape from the tiger that was chasing you through the jungle. In our current world, much of our anxiety comes from stress, which is not necessarily perilous or life-threatening. Any stress will keep the body in a heightened state of adrenaline production for long periods.

Stress is defined as "the level at which any activity causes the body to become stimulated to the point the body is put into peril." This may not be physical peril, but rather an emotional equivalent. For example, you may be scared you are going to lose your job or business. As you become stressed, the body works to overcome and cope with the stress.

We may have become so conditioned to various stressors we frequently encounter on a daily basis, that we may not identify that feeling of stress as a notable event. When the body no longer has the energy reserves to manage the stress and maintain chemical balances, it crosses the *metabolic threshold*. The body's systems: endocrine, circulatory, nervous, digestive, and respiratory react to adrenaline and other substances excreted by the adrenal glands. The body then experiences something like battle mode. It arms itself to perform in the face of stress. The body can only handle so much stress and does so by maintaining the most important and vital bodily functions first. When it can no longer cope, the body's systems shut down, or decrease their ability to function to a certain degree, and the messages that keep the body's internal chemistry in line cannot control the balance any longer.

During this "over achiever" period of my life, I was living off of adrenaline. I was caught in a vicious, never-ending cycle of "fight or flight." That is why after performing at peak capacity all day and ignoring my fatigue and pain, I would feel exhausted and sick. This feeling would last until I could get myself revved up on adrenaline again. Adrenaline was my internal drug.

Sometimes, people seek a similar high by placing themselves at risk with recreational activities such as bungee jumping or skydiving. Some will even confess they become addicted to the rush and thrill. They are adrenaline junkies, and over time, it may take a bigger and bigger thrill to achieve the same rush. I believe many shopaholics are adrenal fatigue sufferers attempting to generate a high or rush from the quest for material items.

In my life, I would rev myself up, or get angry, just to get through a project or to get through a day. I was merely surviving. When your body has been living in a high-adrenaline state due to stress, even an artificially produced stress, eventually you will cease to perform as well as you once did. Then, it will take more effort and extreme circumstance to be able to function. Those with adrenal fatigue often feel they are winding down just like a clock—and that is exactly what I was doing – winding down. The problem compounds over time until it takes control over your life.

Had you met me during this time, you would have never known I had any problems at all and certainly not any health issues. I put on a first-class front. I was the master of looking great on the surface. People would ask how I did it all: care for my beautiful family, dote on my loving husband, and help manage our business. These compliments made me feel that I had them fooled! I was wasting away, but not many people knew. By some convoluted logic, fooling others helped me deal with my problem. I knew I could not control what my body was doing, but I thought I could control how I appeared to others. Controlling my environment and the people in it gave me a sense of control over myself. I even put up a facade to my closest friends. I almost lost some friendships because of this during my long years of suffering. Although my control was an illusion, I was determined to cling to it and keep up the façade, no matter what.

When I did complain, I would feel guilty. I started my sentences to my husband with qualifying statements such as, "Honey, I know I sound so weak but…" Emphatically, I should have said, "Listen up! I feel as if I am slowly dying, and I need help now!" But I could not say that. I did not want to appear out of control, and I felt ashamed and guilty for not feeling 110%.

On occasion, my sister-in-law would call to chat; her life sounded so wonderful. It seemed she was always bubbly and happy -- all the emotions and words I wanted to say, do and be. She had become involved with a multi-level marketing company that promoted a fabulous diet product and energy pill. She would tell me how great she felt and looked because she had slimmed down to a size two. I, on the other hand, was still carrying extra pounds of baby weight. I felt anything but great, and the vision of my losing weight was tempting. Because of my obsessive drive, I theorized that I could fix myself on the outside by taking a little diet pill. I would be thinner, be cured, and then I would be happy.

I had no idea that little pill would fuel the vicious downward spiral in my health. Originally, when I started taking the diet/energy pills I considered myself 20 pounds overweight. Within a few weeks of taking them consistently, my weight dropped so rapidly I could not do anything to slow it down. When I finally stopped taking the diet/energy pills, I had lost twenty-five pounds and had trouble sitting in the bath tub because it hurt so much. The bones of my pelvis compressed my skin when I sat to bathe, causing pain. I was too thin.

The diet/energy pills allowed me to continue my obsessive behavior because they provided a burst of artificial energy. Ultimately, they caused my undiagnosed problem to intensify. It was like tossing gasoline on to burning embers. I discontinued the diet pills and immediately began a vitamin and exercise regimen. I believed I was merely out of shape and not getting proper nutrition, and that I needed vitamins and exercise to improve.

My emotional relationship with my children and husband suffered during this time, as well. My children were everything to me, but I barely had the strength to enjoy them or to provide the emotional stability and support they needed. Sometimes, I would lie on the floor in my kitchen and listen to the sounds of their playing. All I could think of was escaping. If only I could escape from my nightmare, then I could be a 'normal' mother and wife.

My husband and I took several short trips over long weekends. Instead of our trips being romantic, bonding experiences, I would take over-the-counter sleeping pills and watch movies for three days straight. By the time I had returned home, the guilt caused from being away from my children had become overwhelming. This added a whole new problem over which I could obsess and worry. When I was home, all I wanted to do was sleep or get away. Then when I was away, all I wanted to do was go home because of my self-induced guilt. I was a fine mother, but I was very sad and longed to feel what I perceived all other mothers felt.

I honestly wondered if I were missing a specific gene—the "Good Mommy Gene." I imagined it would be a gene that would make me just like other mothers. Maybe I just did not have the capacity to be happy.

I did not realize it may not be my fault if the sound of my child's cry caused me to panic, or if the effort of getting up out of my chair to see what the children were doing would zap all of my inner strength. I forced myself to be on the go every minute. My rationale was that if I stayed up and moving, working on countless projects, using that old faithful friend, adrenaline, then at least I could function.

Even then, I knew something had to give eventually. I tried my best not to dwell on the idea of going to another doctor, but I knew I could not exist in this downward spiral forever. As much as I attempted to focus on the present and get through each day, I had a sense of impending doom. It was as if my car were speeding toward a cliff, and there was nothing I could do to stop it. The worst part was my knowing that this was not the life I was intended to live. I felt cheated, as if someone had stolen my real life and replaced it with this shell of nothingness. No matter what, I was determined to get better, even if that meant trying some unorthodox ideas.

If you fall, fall on your back.
If you can look up, you can
get up.

- Les Brown

Chapter 3

Adrenal Fatigue & Related Syndromes

Once you choose hope,
anything's possible.

- Christopher Reeve

Today, the terms adrenal fatigue, chronic fatigue syndrome (CFS), and fibromyalgia are frequently mentioned in the media and online reports. They are blamed for almost every mysterious and nondescript symptom. Unfortunately, many doctors refuse to acknowledge the group of symptoms as a real syndrome and still think it is psychological. It is not. Some estimate as many as 70%, or more, of individuals with CFS or fibromyalgia have an underlying adrenal condition.

For most sufferers, there is usually a precipitating event that causes major stress in their lives. It could be a change in employment, an illness, the death of a close relative, or as in my case, the birth of a child. Stressors do not necessarily have to be negative events; they are just stressful events that trigger the body's response and prompt it to release adrenaline. Put simply, continued stress is cumulative, and over time the body's response changes until it is not producing enough adrenaline. This causes a disruption in the body's ability to function and creates disabling fatigue along with a host of other symptoms.

Symptoms include low blood pressure, extreme temperature fluctuation, and vacant, hollow eyes. This last symptom is one I can immediately recognize in others, even when meeting complete strangers. I look back at photos of myself during those dark days, and my hollow eyes and vacant stare are obvious. It was as if I were there—but not really there.

Contrary to the opinion of many, adrenal fatigue is not a new syndrome. People have experienced the condition for generations, but many physicians do not recognize it as a distinct and separate problem. While awareness is increasing, lack of knowledge and formal medical acceptance or training in this area make it difficult for a patient to be properly diagnosed and treated. All doctors are familiar with Addison's disease, which occurs when the adrenal glands are not functioning at all, and there are well-known tests to confirm the diagnosis. Unfortunately, these tests do not show a *low* adrenal function; they only determine whether the adrenals are functioning or not.

Life with Adrenal Fatigue

There are a number of distinct patterns in the life of someone with adrenal fatigue. One of the most disturbing is the disruption of sleep. You would think that someone who is exhausted would have no trouble sleeping, but sleep for the adrenal patient can be elusive. I dreaded the night coming. I would lie awake and agonize over possible catastrophes that might afflict my family or friends, and all the while I was trying to will myself to sleep. This unrealistic, obsessive behavior was another symptom of my adrenal fatigue and when coupled with my insomnia would leave me tossing and turning all night.

I knew both my body and mind needed sleep, and that is why I would take over-the-counter sleep aids. I was trying to force my body to rest, but when I would sleep, it was not a restful or renewing sleep. It was as if I were still awake hovering over my body and watching myself all night. I was never deeply sleeping. I have heard this phenomenon referred to as "twilight sleep," a state of floating between true sleep and being fully awake. Sleep was disappointing, and each morning I had to drag myself out of bed. This was out of character for me; I had always been well and energetic. Now, everything was a struggle.

Individuals with adrenal fatigue have specific and identifiable energy patterns. They are usually very tired in the morning and will sleep until after 10:00 a.m. when given the chance, yet they will not feel fully awake until after a noon meal. There is usually a lull in energy between 3:00 and 4:00 p.m., and they feel the need to take a nap. Most people with adrenal fatigue feel better and have more energy between 5:00 and 6:00 p.m., but there can be another lull between 8:00 and 10:00 p.m. From 10:00 p.m. until 2:00 a.m., they experience increased energy and can work at a high level of productivity.

As you have probably guessed, these energy patterns can present a dilemma for people who are expected to work during the day, care for a family, and still be rested and relaxed the next day. I spent years fighting this energy pattern. I forced myself to be up early to get everyone ready and myself to work, but then I had to hit the caffeine during the afternoon and, of course, the over-the-counter sleeping pills at night.

I artificially stimulated myself with a lot of caffeine in an attempt to replicate the energy levels I'd had prior to my daughter's birth, but it just was not working. One of the most prevalent psychological effects was the ceaseless and all-consuming feeling that I was dying. This feeling was more than just knowing something extraordinary was happening within my body. I could sense death hovering right above me like a shadow, and it never left my side. It was just waiting for the signal to attack. No one understood, and I could not convey the strength of my feeling.

It Is More Common Than You Think

Over the past decade, there have been several studies revealing that the prevalence of adrenal fatigue is much higher than previously thought. It has come upon us with the strength of a new epidemic because more people are recognizing the signs and symptoms. Still, the broader medical community has not acknowledged it as the devastating illness it truly is.

In 1993, the Centers for Disease Control and Prevention (CDC) estimated that fewer than 20,000 people in the US had CFS, which includes symptoms of adrenal fatigue. In the late 1990s, however, CDC researchers studied community-based samples and increased their estimation to a little over 0.4%, or approximately 800,000 people. In 1997, researchers from Great Britain stated their community samples indicated as much as 2.6% of the population were affected by these same symptoms. A later study conducted by the CDC in June of 2007 mirrored these results, estimating that 2.54% of the population suffered from this syndrome. This means there are in excess of seven million Americans exhibiting some signs or symptoms of adrenal fatigue.

This is truly an epidemic, and I believe the daily stress of having the constant stimulation of cell phones, computers, and 24/7 news channels intensifies the symptoms. When do we decompress? When do we take our time without the outside world? When our parents were growing up, they did not have the steady stimulation of cell phones, computers, and PDAs, or the stress that comes with having to pay for all of these extras.

The difference between the various studies concerning the percentages of people affected is largely due to the guidelines being used to determine what symptoms are, or are not, related to adrenal fatigue. Though you may not know someone who has been diagnosed with adrenal fatigue, you will know of someone who has not felt well and has been advised by the doctor that the fatigue was due to stress, or to depression. You may have experienced many of the symptoms yourself, from interrupted sleep to specific energy patterns that interfered with your day. Since there are no definitive tests, there is no more accurate way to project the number of sufferers. It seems reasonable to report the number is compelling, easily into the millions, and that most sufferers are misdiagnosed.

This was my experience. Once I was written off by my doctor as having a postpartum problem, I was extremely reluctant to return to another medical doctor. This is when I decided to visit an MD/Naturopath. A naturopath uses natural remedies, such as herbs and diet, to assist the body's natural healing powers. They generally do not rely on surgical techniques or synthetic drugs, and their therapies are complementary to traditional medicine.

The naturopath ordered a comprehensive battery of tests. I never was given a definitive diagnosis, but she firmly suggested my entire body was under attack. She never exactly explained what was attacking my body, but prescribed a variety of homeopathic remedies. I was all for taking or doing anything that would help. It was simple; I would mix an elixir—ten drops of this, two drops of that—stir and swallow. She also recommended weekly vitamin B12 injections and ongoing counseling with her. I cannot blame her for thinking that counseling was necessary because the first time I talked to this doctor, I cried for 45 minutes. The frustration overwhelmed me, and I was resentful for having to find alternatives because my other doctor had not bothered to look for other answers, nor did he believe me. I was also exhausted and so weak that I could hardly hold my baby.

I was treated by the naturopath for three months, and I noticed some improvement, but it was not sustained. She had recommended that each day at home I lie down for 45 minutes at exactly the same time. This may have seemed reasonable since I suffered from tremendous fatigue, but I refused. I knew if I were to lie down at that particular time of day, fatigue would overwhelm me, and I would never be able to pull myself up and complete the tasks my family required. My only hope was to keep moving through those periods of time when my energy was at its lowest.

I had no clue what my real problem was, but through trial and error I found what seemed to keep me going. I created my own comfort zone of obsessive behavior and was afraid of what might happen if I stopped doing those things. This was all to counter what I did not understand about my condition. In fact, these behaviors are typical of the coping mechanisms employed by many adrenal fatigue patients. Because of my obsessive thoughts, I believed the more vitamins I consumed, the better off I would be. I was tossing down handfuls of vitamins. While this did not hurt me, I was pushing my body at such a rate that an entire bottle of B complex vitamins could not have fixed the rapid escalation of my symptoms.

There Is Therapy, and Then There Is *Therapy*

As I moved forward battling to escape fatigue, I did find a therapy that provided some temporary relief: Retail Therapy. Many adrenal patients have something in their lives that charges them with a thrill or rush of excitement. For me, the act of shopping and buying—*the hunt*—created excitement and made me hopeful for a short time. I was attempting to fix myself, and so I would try on all styles of clothing. Clothes made me feel pretty and positive. I often received praise for looking nice, which translated into feeling good for that brief, but fleeting, moment.

I would also make unnecessary purchases. While shopping, I felt distracted, somehow more positive, and hopeful this was going to fix me. Perhaps, the act of buying gave me an adrenaline rush. I suspect that many involved with home-shopping networks, gambling, video games, or thrill seeking behaviors—anything to get the adrenal glands to pump—may be suffering from adrenal fatigue.

When I would shop, it was not about spending money. Instead, it was like being on a hunt. I would look and search, building up to that moment when I found the right item and purchased it. This was the momentum and outer fix I was seeking. At the end of the hunt, I would be exhausted and filled with doubt. Did I need three shirts of the same color?

Some adrenaline patients seem to live their lives in chaos. They may create disputes and obstacles so that they have an issue to get upset about and induce their adrenalin to flow. I have heard discussions about adrenal patients being referred to as "drama queens" because they seem to revel in chaotic lives, due to their need to talk over others' problems and their interest in situations. Possibly, they may be getting an adrenaline fix. Reality TV was made for adrenal patients!

I was determined to live my life in rigid order, just to feel in control and get through the day. Now I realize there were incidents and situations that I made bigger, made worse, or made last longer than necessary.

When I walk through a mall now, I look around and wonder how many of the people I see are adrenal sufferers, and if they are seeking that "high" or creating some chaos in their lives. I wonder if they require that rush, as I once did, to get them going. They may pick a fight with a clerk or call home and argue with a family member. How many people have you seen screaming into their cell phones while walking through the mall? They may have been trying to generate enough adrenaline to make it home.

Meanwhile, my relationships suffered. I was becoming more transparent and was faking it less often. I had begun to open up and talk about my pain and fatigue with those closest to me. I could not seem to hold it together nor relate to anyone on the same level as I had before. I felt so different, and I was so different. I continually worried and felt insecure. I concluded most everyone viewed me as crazy, and that they thought I should just dig deeper and get over it, but I could not. I knew there was more to my problem, but I sensed my complaints were holding less weight with both friends and family. I worried we were growing more distant, and I was harboring a great deal of resentment and self-loathing. Why could I not be like everyone else and enjoy the blessings my life had to offer? Was there something so wrong with me that I was not meant to be happy? How could my husband successfully treat so many people and help them feel better? Why was he not able to help me?

There were more questions than answers. I evolved into a late-night infomercial junky, purchasing anything that might help. I spent thousands on air purifiers just on the chance I was allergic to something in my house. I purchased several super-turbo juicers because I was convinced that if I juiced all my food into a liquid mush, it might make me feel better. I bought self-help systems, workbooks, DVDs, and exercise gizmos. I was desperate for something, anything that might help - even a little bit.

There was a time when I insisted upon purchasing pure, organic shampoo, soap, and detergent, just in case those were causing my problem. Now, this behavior makes me laugh at myself, but I recall determinedly driving across town to the only organic store in the area and buying an awful organic shampoo that looked like mud. My hair was already dull and brittle due to my condition, and after using that stuff it looked like a pathetic greasy rat's nest! Again, I was desperate to try anything.

This was also during the time when black mold in homes was becoming a well-known health issue. Listening to the news report the symptoms, all of which sounded like what I was experiencing, made me paranoid. I hired a contractor to check every nook and cranny of our house, to the point of having him remove baseboards and drywall that were perfectly fine. I put him through that just to be certain there was no mold.

I am certain he speculated that I was unglued the day I burst into tears and cried my eyes out in front of him. I just wanted him to find something—anything—that would explain what was happening. I wanted to prove to everyone that there was something *physically* wrong with me.

Don't be afraid your life will end; be afraid that it will never begin.

- Grace Hansen

Chapter 4

Crossing the Metabolic Threshold

The greatest part of our happiness depends on our dispositions, not our circumstances.

- Martha Washington

People suffering from adrenal fatigue need to understand their bodies can become stimulated to the point of being in peril. This is what I refer to as our "metabolic threshold," and crossing it can create a cascade of problems. The body is an amazing symphony of hormones, enzymes, and biological processes that keeps its chemistry in balance. When the body becomes out of balance, it will strive to produce the right amount of substances to correct the imbalance. Many of these substances are created within the adrenal glands.

The problem for adrenal fatigue patients occurs when the adrenal glands are overstimulated for an extended time. The "metabolic threshold" refers to the stage at which the body overstimulates the adrenal glands and pushes them into overdrive. Over time, as the glands are repeatedly overstimulated, due to stress, the threshold level lowers and the glands become weakened. This means it takes lesser amounts of stress to cause the body to overreact, thus leading to a downward spiral as the glands become more and more fatigued.

Crossing the metabolic threshold can be brought about by events viewed as "normal." Therefore, the patient does not realize the negative effects of these "normal", cumulative stresses. The events can be as minor as arguing with a family member or as major as undergoing surgery. The stressful or traumatic event reduces the body's ability to respond normally, so then it overreacts as if attacked. As these overreactions build up over time, the adrenal glands eventually respond at the most minimal level, leaving the patient partially or completely unable to function normally.

The threshold at which this happens depends upon the stage of adrenal failure the person is experiencing. Adrenal failure moves through several stages, as described by Dr. Gerald Poesnecker in his book, *Mastering Your Life*. As your body progresses through each escalating stage, the adrenal glands weaken. This means it takes less and less stress to drain the person's energy, and the result is exhaustion. This progression occurs at different rates for everyone, but the symptoms are largely the same.

The problem with adrenal fatigue is the adrenal glands are frequently over stimulated throughout the course of daily living; therefore, it is hard to recognize. At first, the adrenal glands bounce back. This enables the stressed person to keep going, even though they are exhausted. The adrenals have back-up reserves that allow a person to continue past their normal stress load, like reserve battery power. When you sleep, these reserves are replenished. When you are in a state of continual stimulation, the body does not have time to rest and recharge. Soon, these reserves become depleted.

It is like partially charging a battery. If you continue to do this, the battery becomes weaker and weaker. The adrenal glands are the same. When they cannot fully recharge, they weaken. Eventually, they can cease to function normally.

Stages of Adrenal Fatigue

In the first stage, many people know they do not feel right but cannot come up with a reason why. Their adrenal glands do not produce enough of two substances, cortisol and DHEA, to keep the body functioning properly. These people appear anxious, suffer from insomnia, have heart palpitations, and possibly experience panic attacks. This is usually the stage at which patients first see their doctor. They cannot sleep, have nightmares, and feel their heart racing for no reason. I had all of these symptoms. For me, as well as for many others, the most destructive symptom was the inability to sleep.

These symptoms drive most patients to their doctor's office, where generally they are prescribed sleep aids or antidepressants. Ironically, these medications can be perceived by the body as being traumatic, so patients often experience the drugs' side-effects, but not their benefits. This is because the body feels as if it is under attack and fights the medications. This means patients are taking sleeping aids but still not sleeping.

The next manifestation of the syndrome is one most adrenal sufferers report as being the definitive moment they knew something was seriously wrong. I know firsthand that this experience is horrible. The psychological effects brought on by lack of sleep and imprisoning fatigue become all consuming. The overwhelming sense of dread and impending doom become daily companions. As the cortisol levels climb, the adrenal glands produce DHEA to compensate.

This syndrome is a progression and intensification of these same symptoms, but soon DHEA levels begin to fall. Rather than this being an indication that the patient is improving, it actually shows that the body's ability to produce stress hormones is decreasing.

Unfortunately, these hormones vary during the day. Thus, even if a physician were to test a person's hormone levels, the results would only indicate the levels at the specific time of the test. In other words, results would not reflect the overall trend. Most medical doctors view these hormones as existing within a range. This range can vary considerably and the results can still be classified as being in a normal range.

Well into the advancement of adrenal failure, the classic symptom of ongoing, debilitating fatigue appears. Previously, the patient may have had many symptoms on and off, and now they are constant. This stage is noteworthy, because the patient's desperation has escalated to the point they will try about anything to get well. Unfortunately, many of the cures and remedies will continually breach the metabolic threshold and continue to stress the adrenals. Other physical problems soon manifest.

These problems could be in the form of dental conditions such as your gums may bleed, or you may develop infections or abscesses. In my case, even though I had an impeccable record of seeing my dentist, I had three root canals and many fillings. Also, your skin becomes dry. This is especially noticeable on the bottoms of your feet, which can dry out and crack and bleed. My heels were terrible and resembled the Mojave Desert. Frequent urination and the feeling I could not completely empty my bladder, especially at night, was another problem that kept me awake and added to my feeling of panic. I experienced incessant and unexplained nausea, and I was weak and lightheaded when I stood too quickly.

A most disconcerting symptom is fuzzy thinking and not being able to remember. It was disturbing to me when someone would ask for my social security number or a telephone number because I would draw an absolute blank. One day I was driving to the office, using the same route I had driven for years, and I suddenly realized I did not know where I was, or even that I was in the state of Indiana. Somehow, I remembered my mom's telephone number, and I knew she was my mom. I called her sobbing and begging her to tell me what to do. My mom had to tell me to pull over and get off the road. I did, and as I sat slumped in the car crying into the phone, I spotted a road sign I recognized. I knew where I was. I suddenly snapped back into reality. Some adrenal patients have been paralyzed by the fear that they may be experiencing early onset dementia or other memory related diseases when it is really an adrenal problem.

These mental changes are due to changes in body chemistry, nothing more. As time passes and cortisol levels continue to drop, the patient becomes more and more sensitive to everything, including bright lights and smells. Chemical smells, perfume, and even certain foods (like onions) can leave an adrenal patient reeling.

Few people move into full-blown adrenal failure. This is the stage when the body becomes almost unable to cope with any stress. The adrenal glands are only marginally functional, and the patient is nearly debilitated by fatigue. They are unable to cope with anything or anyone, and even the slightest stimulation may leave them completely incapacitated. They tend to become reclusive and unable to interact with the outside world. Since the adrenals control function of some vital organs and processes such as regulating blood pressure, without urgent medical care these patients could eventually die.

Metabolic Events

As each person travels his or her road through adrenal fatigue, they can look back and recall the specific metabolic events that precipitated their worsening symptoms. I experienced many of the common events, of which the following are just a few. You will have specific events unique to you, but as you recognize them, you will be able to avoid those that worsen your symptoms.

1. Change in Diet – Many of us do not eat well in the first place, but when we choose to make an abrupt change in our eating habits, it can cause us to breach our metabolic threshold and bring on an episode of extraordinary fatigue. For example, I bought a juicer from a late-night infomercial. Many people juice and experience wonderfully improved nutrition and health. This was not the case for me. I continually juiced according to the recommendations, but I became more fatigued. My body was not coping with the change, and I felt wretched. A similar adverse reaction can occur if you take diet pills (did that too), drink herbal teas, or take herbal supplements. This does not mean any of these are bad in and of themselves, but for the adrenal patient they can be devastating because the body is hypersensitive. Compounding these issues is the fact that we often do several of them at the same time, thus intensifying their effects. How often have you started a new diet and taken new supplements at the same time? We all have made numerous changes at the same time, but for those with adrenal fatigue this can be disastrous. When implementing changes, introduce one element at a time and journal your changes so you can determine which ones help and which ones do not.

2. Physical changes – If you have had surgery, delivered a child, or had some other medical procedure, your metabolic threshold may be breached due to the physical or emotional stress placed upon your body. It may be

a major trauma such as from an accident, or it may be relatively minor, such as a visit to your dentist. This is especially true, if doctors do not understand the fragile state of adrenal patients. Anything that initiates change may kick the adrenal glands into high gear, and if the glands are too weak to respond, the body will have a difficult time keeping up with the energy required. The body does not have to be cut open for a problem to arise. Problems can be the result of an illness or perhaps a situation that should be positive, such as needed weight loss. It can take a great deal of energy for the body to adjust to changes. Sometimes it is just too much.

3. Scents – It may seem strange to think that certain smells can breach your metabolic threshold, but it is true. The smell of onions was a big problem for me. Onions would immediately generate an almost violent reaction, and I would become physically ill. Many adrenal patients are aggravated by fragrances and odors from perfumes, lotions, foods, or industrial chemicals. These sensitivities can increase, and additional scents may cause an adverse response.

4. Drugs – Many of the drugs we take for granted, including many over-the-counter drugs, can breach the metabolic threshold. This is especially true as the patient becomes more sensitive. Antidepressants, some supplements, and simple flu remedies can bring on extreme fatigue. I include caffeine in this category, because I consider caffeine to be a drug, even though many may not agree. Anything that has the power to stimulate the body is a potential danger to an adrenal patient, and caffeine is a common culprit. This includes

chocolate. Chocolate contains caffeine, as do many other foods and beverages. It is necessary for adrenal patients to carefully examine labels and avoid any stimulant. It can be easy to spot an adrenal sufferer by the number of coffee cups and chocolate wrappers on their desk.

5. Emotional Events – Our emotions are capable of producing changes in the body. Fear is one of the most basic emotions and one that has the ability to produce excessive adrenal activity. The interesting point about feeling an emotion such as fear is that the body does not distinguish between a real or an imagined fear. This means the anxiety and panic attacks many people suffer during the early stages of adrenal fatigue intensifies the problem and creates an endless cycle. I experienced this myself. For example, I would lie awake at night and imagine my children swimming. Then, I would see their little heads going under the water. I would panic because I could not reach them in time. This fear pushed my adrenal glands into hyper-drive which, in turn, made my symptoms worse. There are also unexpected emotional events, such as the death of a loved one, that breach the metabolic threshold and can start anyone on the road to adrenal fatigue. As the fatigue progresses, depression can intensify the emotional stress.

6. External Events – We all have responsibilities and lists of tasks that must be done every day. Any activity has the potential to breach the metabolic threshold. It may be the stress of traffic one day or a large project assigned to be finished by the next day. The adrenal glands respond to each event. Even events such as parties or gatherings can cause a state of excitement or anxiety, which may

lead to stress. Unfortunately, short of living in a plastic bubble, we all encounter everyday stress. From sick kids to a car that will not start, these normal events cause stress and can contribute to adrenal fatigue.

7. People – This is a tough category. We interact with those we love, and with those we do not, every day. Some people will annoy, irritate, and just plain anger us—and those may even be the people we love! Inevitably, there will be people in your life who are the purveyors of doom in many circumstances. They might visit or call you, but either way, they emotionally stress or depress you. These are "energy vampires," and they can suck the life from you, leaving you exhausted and drained. You will have to find ways to guard yourself and protect your emotions in order to move forward.

While it would be advantageous to assemble a complete list of every possible situation that might cause a problem for an adrenal patient, it is an impossible task, because we are all unique. However, just being aware that you have a metabolic threshold and what generally might cause an issue, gives you the awareness to begin monitoring your own situation.

Much of what I have learned on my own journey was through trial and error. Even when I knew there were activities and jobs that I should avoid, I often did them. I am uncertain if I was in denial or if I was hoping things would be fine. Eventually, I learned to listen to my body's needs. As much as I would have liked to have believed I was strong enough, or stubborn enough to overcome, at this point my body won. When you have something physically wrong, even though you have significant mental strength, it is hard to overcome. You must address the issue and fix the problem.

Much of my personal struggle included convincing other people that there was something wrong. Even though I intuitively knew I was right, a seed of doubt was planted when I was dismissed by medical professionals and told my problems were all in my mind. As I gained awareness and recognized what worsened my symptoms, there were times I purposely exposed myself to stimuli just to prove I was right—and I was right despite the disbelief of many. My own instincts pulled me through my darkest hours, and those instincts are all many adrenal patients have to cling to when no one else understands.

When the world says, "Give up," Hope whispers, "Try it one more time."

- Author Unknown

Chapter 5

The Emotion of Frustration

It's not the load that breaks you down, it's the way you carry it.

- Lena Horne

Arguably, the most difficult aspect of adrenal fatigue is the variety of emotions you experience while you are suffering, while you are seeking answers, and while you are recovering. Some of these emotions are due to the reactions of others when they offer flippant suggestions such as, "get more sleep" or "snap out of it." However, the majority of the negative emotions are self-inflicted. You wonder: what is wrong with *me*, why do *I* not feel happiness, and why is this happening to *me*. I remember numerous times I asked my husband during my bleakest hours, "Are you sure aliens do not come into our room at night and suck the life out of me?" That should tell you how desperate I was. I would believe and hang on to any explanation, even if that explanation included little green men from Mars! When you have others doubting you and your so-called condition, your mind and soul will search for anything.

For me, the most devastating emotion was the guilt I experienced when I could not feel the happiness of mothering my children, or when I felt little or no emotion toward those I loved. When I would listen to my sister-in-law sharing her wonderful life, I was numb. This made me feel worse. Not only did I feel *no emotion* for her good fortune, I felt *no emotion* for mine. This inability to feel joy and happiness is a vicious cycle and can make you believe you are a cold and terrible person. In my situation, this led to me having feelings of anger toward myself and confusion as to why I seemed singled out to be affected.

In an effort to act as though you feel better than you do, you may emulate someone you view as a better parent than you by enrolling your children in the same activities as their children and by going through the same motions. I did this hoping I would be able to feel better but it didn't work. I still felt dreadful and was willing to try almost anything to make my life seem better. A humorous example of me attempting to physically appear just like a particular mom I admired was when I bought a similar sweater. Her sweater had a snowman appliqué. Mine had a Santa. That was not even my style. I do not have a closet full of sweaters with dancing reindeer and elves on them! I believed my friend was the best mom ever, and yes, she looked cute in her little snowman sweater. So the next week I wore my sweater, and in my twisted and emotional jumble, I had hoped if I could emulate her, then I would feel better…like her.

I had a wonderful life with an unbelievable husband and beautiful children. I was a hard worker and had accomplished some of the major goals in my life, but nothing could break through my brain-fog. It did not matter how much I slept or "took it easy," the fatigue was insatiable, and the darkness of the void was emotionally relentless. I was like an empty crater in the center of my universe. I felt *nothing*.

Now you can understand why it is so difficult when doctors misdiagnose adrenal fatigue and categorize the symptoms as stemming from some level of an emotional problem. This supports the adrenal patient's worst fears, and the diagnosis is dead wrong. Many patients are diagnosed with clinical depression, bi-polar disorder, or other severe emotional issues. Or they may be diagnosed with a mild or temporary hormonal imbalance such as postpartum as I was in the beginning. This adds to the guilt the patient feels because their symptoms are being discounted as emotional issues. Rather than understanding this is a biochemical problem within the body, patients are made to feel they can overcome the problem if only they should *desire* to overcome it. This is destructive because these patients cannot feel better by force of will, nor can they seem to convince others of how desperately they long to be better.

Early in my search for a reason, I just needed the doctors to find something concrete—anything—even if it were a bad diagnosis. I knew my problems were not all in my mind, but I wanted confirmation. I would have accepted any physical diagnosis, because I knew that if they found a physical cause, then I could be treated and recover. In an effort to explain to my husband, I would say, "I wish I had a broken arm—then I could show the tangible proof. Then I could tell people, *Look, I am broken; I am wearing a cast*." That is the frustration I felt.

When my concerns were pushed aside and dismissed by physicians, I felt demeaned and humiliated. The last thing I wanted was to be continuously sick, but how could I convince anyone else there was a problem when the doctor was certain the problem was emotional? Because I had become a self-doubter, at the doctor's urging, I agreed to additional counseling sessions, but I considered it a waste of time. One visit, I suddenly flew up out of the "counseling" chair, with tears falling, and shook my finger at her. I wept, "It is *not* in my mind. It is *not* my husband. It is *not* my life. Whether you know it or not, there is something else, entirely, wrong." She would never consider the possibility. She did not believe me and would not listen. I never went back.

Family and friends can unknowingly add to the feelings of guilt and sorrow. Many of us have people in our lives who love us and would do anything for us. Even their patience and tolerance can wear thin when you are sick, day after day and month after month. Even those closest to you may question if you are indeed sick or if there are other reasons behind your behavior. The opinion of the doctor is as much of a validation of the fears of these loved ones, as it is a dismissal of your real, yet underlying, condition. The doctor often speculates the problem is emotionally based, which supports their suspicion that there is not a genuine medical problem after all. At that juncture, some people in your life may be less sympathetic toward you and your symptoms, because they do not believe your problems are real.

This happened to me. When the doctor diagnosed me with postpartum depression, my family assumed this was temporary and soon would pass—but it did not. My mother was with me a lot during this time, and she rejected the doctor's opinion, but why would anyone else? My husband was very understanding, as he thought I was suffering from postpartum depression. But he had a new practice to run, and I was not able to be there to help mentally. To be honest, I felt resentment toward him, because he is a doctor. As a doctor of chiropractic, he helped people every day. They came in to him with pain and concern and then left feeling better. Why couldn't he help me? Why could that not be me?

There were many times I let my friends and family down. There were times I would attend birthday parties for 30 minutes and leave. Sometimes I would not show up at all. We would plan a vacation for months, and then I would cancel at the last minute because my fear of flying overcame me. With adrenal fatigue, you may become fearful of normal activities you once handled with ease.

To this day, I can vividly recall a major letdown I perpetrated upon my family. I am certain those involved still do not understand. My sister-in-law was coming with her family from a long distance for a visit. Because I felt so sick and was well past exhausted, my husband and I decided it would be best to have them cancel their trip. At the very last moment, my husband made that dreaded call and told them they could not come. This was one of the hardest decisions we had ever had to make. Of course, they were extremely upset, which added to my stress from guilt and worry. We had no choice, because I had been having a difficult time with my blood pressure not even registering on a blood pressure monitor: it was dangerously low. Looking back, we should have explained to them exactly what was going on with me, but truthfully we did not have the strength to explain this silent, no-proof, offender. We were afraid this would sound like another excuse, because we were continually canceling plans.

There are many people struggling with adrenal fatigue who do not have adequate support systems. They may be alone, or they may have family and friends who do not understand. I am here to tell you that despite the circumstances, you must believe in yourself. You must know what you feel is real, no matter what your doctor may initially say. You are not crazy, and you are not hopeless. You *can* get better.

One myth about those who suffer from adrenal fatigue is that they cannot hold a job. In my experience, the opposite is true—most sufferers hold down jobs. Some of those jobs create high stress and require high energy, which compounds the problem. There were times, I recall working in an energetic flurry of activity, only to crash and require days of recovery. I relate this to trying to get up the strength to run right through a brick wall, and then later feeling the residual damage. Unfortunately, many people cannot afford to crash or take days off; they must continue with their lives. They lean on any of the multitude of caffeinated beverages and energy drinks available. We are a Red Bull™ generation, but these artificial enhancements can compound the feeling of manic production, followed by a debilitating lack of energy. Adrenal fatigue sufferers could be compared to a functional alcoholic, in that adrenal fatigue patients can generally manage their condition and keep it together and function during working hours, but are fatigued to the point of exhaustion later.

I believe adrenal fatigue sufferers learn to mask their problems. Many do everything they can to appear normal, faking their way through life as I did, although they frequently fail. Those around you can observe there is a problem, but they avoid confronting it as much as you do—especially if they feel there is nothing they can do to help. If you are not affecting their lives, they probably would rather not think about it. Often friends and family members have preconceived assumptions about this condition because of information they have heard or read. They have no understanding of how horrible and trapped it makes you feel, and human nature will take over, and foolish assumptions and words will come rushing out. I would find comfort in promising myself, "I will never have preconceived opinions about anyone's life or problems ever again."

I have also met people who do believe they have the answers: "If you would only eat properly, dig down a little deeper, or exercise." While diet and exercise do have positive effects, the effects may be very different for those suffering from adrenal fatigue. I have found myself gazing at my television while a master workout guru was promoting one of the “feel good, feel great” products or systems. You know the ones. These types just do not get it. Not all things can be solved by more exercise! I had envisioned making them into a speed bump. I want all those with adrenal fatigue to understand —what works for others may not work for you. I have purchased treadmills and a recumbent bike, only to be too physically drained even to sit or stand on them, let alone workout on them.

I look back and laugh at the late night infomercials that lured me into hoping. Some products I bought have never been opened. If the pitch man even implied their products would help me, I was dialing!

Another aspect I want to address is the idea of becoming well in a week or two. Once you understand your condition, you will realize that is a false concept. I have no illusions about recovery and living with adrenal fatigue. I wish to be objective and say that recovery may take years. I recall sitting in a clinic in Pennsylvania and listening to the doctor say to me, “The moment you realize this is going to take years and when you stop fighting against it, will be the moment you will have some peace and begin your recovery.” His comments made me livid, and I began to sabotage my experience. I was not ready to hear that this could not be fixed quickly.

You may not be ready to accept these words either. I am writing this book for you to read when you are alone, desperate, and ready to accept your condition. I will be here to walk with you all the way. You can have a much better life. Life may not be a perfect reflection of the classic American super-mom or dad, yet it can be a fulfilling life. You will feel better, you will have peace, and you will begin your recovery. However, living with adrenal fatigue is a lifelong understanding of how your body works and what events will trigger your adrenal glands. There is no quick fix, but you can recover your life.

This is one of the problems some patients have—it takes too long to get well. We are an instant gratification society. We want it now, and we want it EASY. In reality, it is not that recovery takes too long; it is the lack of understanding that recovering your health is a lifelong pursuit. You do not just figure it out, adjust a few points, and then never have a reoccurring problem. Once you know you suffer from adrenal fatigue and recognize what triggers your symptoms, you will understand that the potential is always there to cross your metabolic threshold, and so you must be ever vigilant.

You have to commit to the process of becoming better, in order to feel better. Recovery is not a one-shot deal; it is a lifestyle. I picture recovery as being similar to balancing the chemistry of water in a swimming pool. My neighbor has a perfect pool, but my pool may be green some days for no apparent reason. You need to treat your pool each day with specific supplements that maintain balance. Who knows why some pools are clear and others become green and soupy? All we do know is a green and soupy pool is not going to fix itself. It will take some work, some patience, and some persistence. You cannot fall into the trap of comparing yourself to those who do not have adrenal fatigue. You are different and may always be different. Therefore, you will have to take certain steps to improve your health that others may not have to take.

A common assumption is that since adrenal fatigue is primarily due to stress; men are more prone to the problem. It was once labeled as "burnout," a term which was popular in the 1980s. Some attributed it to buckling under the pressure of the corporate environment, but this was really the first generation of people to be bombarded with stress on every level of their daily lives, and this stress was the real culprit. Yes, men do experience this problem. Although some are too embarrassed to admit they are suffering. Still, the majority of suffers do tend to be women.

The adrenal glands regulate a number of hormones, and these hormones have a greater impact on women—especially in times of intense stress like pregnancy and childbirth. Many women are also the "quarterback" pivot of their family, keeping everything and everyone running on time and on schedule. Ongoing stress at home can be more poisonous than anything the working environment can produce. There are amazing expectations of women today, and many of these expectations we place upon ourselves. We want to be excellent wives, and we want to be outstanding mothers. Yet, if we are too tired and drained, we can be neither of these. This is hard to accept, especially for someone like me who is a consummate overachiever. I was convinced there were no excuses, and if someone wanted to excel, then all they had to do was work harder. Now when I work with people, I remember we are all individuals born into this world with unique strengths and weaknesses. I want to take the good and understand the more challenging aspects. I cannot control others, but I can control how I respond or choose not to respond to them.

I wanted to be a loving mother, but I struggled to muster the energy to hold my child, and always felt as if I should be doing more for her. I remember lying on the couch hoping

I would have the energy to function for a few hours when my husband came home. More often than not, I failed. I was fooling no one but myself. Many adrenal patients have an experience they would point to as when they realized they had hit bottom. A time that they will invariably remember—and may even regret. My rock bottom was the night of my children's tee-ball game. My husband knew we had a game and had been calling me during the day to discuss our plans. Every minute that passed, I sank deeper and deeper into fatigue. I was a frequent no-show for games, and I knew he was pushing me to make this one.

Around 5:00 p.m., I could barely walk to the bathroom because of my fatigue. Each step would cause my heart to pound and flutter. I was lying in bed with such fear and desperation that all I wanted to do was thrash around the bed. I was exhausted, yet I had an overpowering restlessness. My husband came home expecting me to be up and ready, but I was not. I begged him to stay home and not to go. I knew he felt trapped, and he did not want to be one of those parents who never follows through on promises to their children. He went to the game, and I lay in our bed. I kept the TV on for background noise so I would not have to endure the engulfing silence of the house.

I was staring out over the tops of the trees surrounding the lake, and I could see an outline of a beam of light shining into my darkened bedroom. The light came straight toward me in my bed. As I lay there, I prayed, "God, will you help me?" I begged and cried in desperation. Slowly, I sensed a warm blanket of peace surround me. I remember feeling: I am alone, I am at peace, and I am dying. Believe it or not, I was at peace with the idea of dying. It was okay. I stretched across my bed and reached for the telephone. I called my Mom. I whispered, "Mom, I am dying." I cannot imagine ever receiving that call from my child, but my mom stayed with me, on the phone, until my husband came home. It was the absolute low for me. I had to do something.

You cannot pretend forever, and at some point in time your body will shut you down. You cannot be rich enough, well connected enough, or accomplished enough to escape this problem. Adrenal fatigue is an equal-opportunity destroyer.

Numerous people believe all that is required to increase your energy is to detoxify with a seven-day cleanse or through fasting. Detoxifying the body takes energy. By shocking your system with these techniques, you can easily exceed your metabolic threshold and feel even worse. You must understand that the supplements and diets others find helpful may be counterproductive for those who suffer adrenal fatigue.

I also have had people offer advice such as, "If you could just start acting happier, then you would feel better." Adrenal fatigue does not work that way. You cannot pretend to feel better and expect your body follow along. In fact, you are probably having trouble controlling fear and negative thoughts anyway. In addition, your energy system is not working effectively. No matter how hard you work to convince yourself that you are getting better, you will not *feel* better until you take the steps to improve the underlying chemical imbalance.

The good news is there are several actions you can take to feel better now. These do not require you to take medication or visit a herd of doctors. You can take control of your life. Whether you have the support from loved ones, or not, your future health is your responsibility. You cannot let others determine what is, or is not, wrong with you based on missed diagnoses and wrong assumptions.

If you are alone, I will be with you. If you need encouragement, know I have walked in your shoes and have come out on the other side. Decide now to take those first steps to real healing.

Being happy doesn't mean that everything is perfect. It means that you've decided to look beyond the imperfections.

- Anonymous

Chapter 6

The First Steps

Patience and perseverance have a magical effect before which difficulties disappear and obstacles vanish.

- John Quincy Adams

Once you become aware of the underlying adrenal fatigue, there is often a period when you might be in denial or refuse to accept there is no quick fix. Eventually, you must accept the facts, if you are to improve your health.

Do not be put off if you do not fall within someone else's norm, because a norm merely represents an average, so do not carry the preconceived idea that you are trying to hit a particular number or fall within a specific range on a test. Because we are all different, it is impossible for anyone to tell you exactly what will or will not lessen the effects of adrenal fatigue for you. There are, however, some broad generalizations that can be made and certain areas to try first.

One of the more difficult aspects of adrenal fatigue is putting the pieces together. This is because everything can have an effect on you. This includes what you eat, what you drink, how much sleep you get, if you exercise (and how much), how busy your schedule is, and with whom you spend your time. It is much like piecing together a giant puzzle, but I think this problem is much more complex than a giant puzzle . It is similar to solving a Rubik's Cube because in the beginning there seems to be infinite possibilities and each move affects all of the others.

The best way to understand your personal situation, and solve your own puzzle, is to keep a journal. This journal will include the things you eat and drink, the activities in which you engage, and your encounters with people. This will also allow you to record how each of these has made you feel. Because adrenal fatigue is influenced by every aspect of life, it requires more than just watching what you eat—although food plays a large role. Here is an example of journaling:

Date: June 1, 2010	Event/Food	Result
6:30 a.m.		Woke with dry eyes and a headache
7:30 a.m.	Bagel w/ cream cheese/coffee	Next two hours had to push myself to get anything done
12:30 p.m.	Turkey Swiss panini/iced tea	Next day felt a little off
3:00 p.m.	Iced tea	Feel a little foggy like I need a nap
4:00 p.m.	Meeting at work	Very short tempered with colleague—unjustified
6:00 p.m.	Baked chicken and asparagus	
7:00 p.m.	Sister called to talk about marital problems	Felt completely drained and overly tired

In addition to these notations, you will also want to keep a regular and frequent note of your blood pressure, pulse, and blood sugar—all of which can be monitored easily and quickly at home using devices found at your local drug store. This will allow you to track trends within your body and learn how it responds to certain items or events.

This chart is just one example of a journal; yours can be more or less detailed. However, more details will aid you in determining what foods or situations are contributing to your problem. For example, after eating any food with onion I was exhausted. According to one doctor, onions can have this effect on many adrenal patients. However, without tracking in my journal, it would have been very difficult to discover that onions were a problem.

I call this the "guess and test" method. Keep track, and this will be an effective way to improve your health, in the short term, as you learn what to avoid. While people, activities, and diet are the three main areas of concern, the biggest, for most people, is diet.

Many people experience a significant improvement when they switch to an organic diet. You may be wondering how this could make a difference, but it can make a difference because "Organic" foods are grown without herbicides, pesticides, and are preserved without additives. Since organic foods are typically more expensive, many people avoid them and feed their families regular produce and processed foods, but there can be consequences.

The majority of food today contains herbicides and pesticides, which are used to produce the best looking fruit and vegetables possible. Pretty produce sells better so this is a priority for producers and grocers even if it means they are not as healthy. Synthetic hormones are also used to maximize plant and animal growth. These substances are bad for you and can affect your body in negative ways. Many people's bodies do not show obvious and immediate effects from these substances, because the body has an incredible ability to overcome toxins. But remember, adrenal fatigue patients are more sensitive to these contaminants.

Another factor affecting our food supply is the fact that most seeds used to grow our food, or grow grain to feed the animals we use for food, are genetically altered and infused with toxins. One type of seed treatment is known as "Round-Up Ready", meaning the seed has been altered to make it resistant to the active ingredient in herbicides. These and other chemical additives migrate into our food and drain into our water supply. Even though most vegetables, fruits and meats contain only small amounts of these chemicals, they concentrate within our bodies as we ingest more and more over the course of our lifetime. Organic foods ensure that these chemicals are nonexistent at the seed level, and ensure none are added as the plants grow and mature.

The idea that eating organic is much too expensive is a myth many believe today. Decades ago, organic foods were harder to find and they were more expensive. However, today there are entire organic groceries, and most major grocery chains offer organic products at reasonable prices, simply because of the greater demand. Even Wal-Mart offers a great variety of organic foods. This means you can feed your entire family tasty and healthful food for about the same price as nonorganic food.

Food Allergies

Many people suffer from food allergies. According to a recent survey by the National Institute of Health, the incidences of food allergies in children have increased 18% between 1996 and 2006. In our current environment of better healthcare and knowledge of the body, it seems counterintuitive that we should be experiencing such an explosion of allergic reactions to our food. One has to ask, "So, what has changed?" Previous generations did not have such widespread allergies, and even those who did have allergies did not exhibit such violent reactions. These reactions force us to look at the food supply to determine what has changed about the food we consume today.

A significant difference in our food supply over the last 15 years has been the introduction of genetically engineered foods. Genetic engineering is the process through which scientists remove genes representing beneficial properties from one plant (such as resistance to certain pests) and insert them into another plant to achieve those same properties. On the surface, this seems as if this would improve our food supply, but when you mix genes you can never accurately predict unintentional outcomes.

One example of this was a variety of corn introduced in 1999, called StarLink. This engineered variety contained a "Bt" protein that gave the corn resistance to a devastating type of caterpillar. The company that invented the corn, Aventis (based in France), was confident the corn would be approved for human consumption and contracted with US farmers to start growing crops of StarLink. Unfortunately, the "Bt" protein also alters the way the human body digests the corn, which can produce more pronounced allergic reactions. For this reason, approval was denied.

The EPA did not approve StarLink for human consumption, but because growers either did not realize this, or just mistakenly put the corn into the wrong bins, the corn ended up in our food supply anyway. In 2000, Kraft recalled taco shells marketed under the Taco Bell brand because there were numerous complaints of severe allergic reactions. The taco shells were found to contain StarLink corn. Even though the product and existing supplies were recalled, several million bushels of StarLink corn were left unaccounted for by the government.

Subsequent tests performed by the EPA in 2000 indicated that as much as 20% of the nation's corn supply for human consumption had been contaminated with this genetically altered corn. Even a decade later, trace amounts can still be found in many corn products. This incident highlights the fact that when our food is genetically altered, even with the best of intentions, unintended consequences emerge that can be devastating to our health.

As we have seen recently in the news, once a problem enters our food supply there is the potential for significant consequences. We have seen recalls of fresh vegetables, such as green onions and spinach, because of pesticides and bacterial outbreaks like salmonella and E-coli. The same is true for processed foods, such as the recent recall of crackers containing contaminated peanut butter.

One of the more insidious issues for me, as a mother, is the practice of injecting dairy cows with hormones and other drugs that alter their body chemistry. Cows are also fed genetically altered grains and a plethora of synthetic and altered hormones, all of which result in the production of genetically engineered milk. I am convinced this is a major reason many of our children develop lactose allergies. If they consume contaminated or altered milk when they are young, how can they be expected to grow and thrive? The saddest aspect of these changes is that there is no requirement or standard for accurately labeling genetically engineered foods. This means that unless you eat entirely organic, you are consuming genetically altered foods.

I am not intimating that one bite of genetically engineered food will cause adrenal fatigue, but the foods we consume have a direct effect on us. We have to assume our body will react to food that has been altered. In order to eliminate as much of the problem as possible, I suggest people eat totally organic and make good notes in their journal if they experience any differences. After a few weeks, you will be amazed by how much better you feel and by how much better the food tastes. One of the discounted side effects of engineering bigger, perfect-looking produce is that it is tasteless. While organic may not be as pretty, the fresh flavor is well worth the effort.

I soak fruits and vegetables in a mixture of lemon juice and filtered water for 20-30 minutes and then rinse. I may cut them up later when I have a burst of energy. Cutting and properly storing them in your refrigerator ensures a healthy snack is available when you are feeling horrible. I cannot tell you the number of days I prepared our dinner at lunch, just to be certain it was ready in case my energy level dropped. Make a plan to keep healthy foods in your home, and then clean them and store them in containers for quick and easy access. I know it is hard to stick to healthy eating when your blood sugar drops and you can hardly think. Planning ahead will improve your ability to make the best choices.

Water

Water, much like the food we eat, is taken for granted. Most municipal water systems contain trace amounts of heavy metals, pesticides, and other chemicals. In 2005, the Environment Working Group, a non-profit company, tested the tap water in 42 states and found some 260 substances. Their findings showed that 141 of these substances have no safety standards for human consumption. How do we know these substances are safe? While amounts of harmful substances in drinking water may be within the "safe" range according to regulators, no amount of a deadly substance is safe. These substances have a greater effect on the young, old, and the immune-compromised population. These substances can also have an effect on someone with adrenal fatigue because the body's chemistry is in such a fragile state.

Many water authorities also add chemicals to water. These additives may include phosphates to inhibit the rusting of water pipes or chlorine to discourage bacteria. Some water supplies come from lakes that have had increased salinity because of drought. In one area of Texas, when the water level of a particular lake that the city draws most of its water from is too low, residents who are sensitive to salt content (or have medical conditions) are advised not to drink the water.

It is a healthy habit to drink filtered tap water or filtered bottled water. I urge you to confirm that the bottle's label shows "filtered," because some of the water used is not filtered and still contains contaminates. Another caution is not to assume you are safe when you drink well-water. Farm and lawn chemicals can, and do, leach through the soil, and our underground water becomes more and more contaminated every year. Standard water tests do not determine the full range of chemicals that might exist, as they usually test only for the most common contaminates.

When you filter your water at home, it is important to use a reverse osmosis system and keep the filters changed regularly. Even using a filtering pitcher for your water, or attaching a filter to your main tap, is an improvement if you cannot invest in a complete filtration system.

Drinking adequate amounts of water is essential for recovery. You need to drink eight 8 oz. glasses each day, and some experts recommend drinking one-half of your body weight in water each day. However, common sense must prevail with that recommendation.

For anyone suffering from adrenal fatigue, monitoring what you take into your body and how it affects you is of major importance. Your body is already weakened, and you need excellent sources of energy. It is time to start replenishing your energy with foods that will build you up, and avoid those to which you have an adverse reaction. Each of us travels this path to recovery in bursts—you will experience a time when you are feeling well and then rationalize, "Well, perhaps I can have some bacon, and maybe it will not affect me this time." Inevitably, we all discover that eating foods we love is frustrating because they often do not love us back.

I love to take my children out for ice cream, but every time I eat the ice cream, I will experience heart palpitations. Now, we make homemade ice cream with organic products. It is a bit more work, but if this means I keep up with my family, and they are not plagued by complaints of my metabolic threshold, this is a better option.

You must choose. You can either feel better or you can continue to deny that part of the problem is that you have not learned what your body needs. This takes time and effort, but the rewards are great. You *can* function normally without feeling horrible and exhausted. That is the goal, right?

Healing is a matter of time,
but it is sometimes also a
matter of opportunity.

- Hippocrates

Chapter 7

Is My Body the Enemy?

Good thoughts are half of good health.

\- Proverb: Yugoslav

As I struggled to recover and improve my health, there were many times it seemed as if my body were working against me. I would improve for a short time, and then within a few weeks I would feel miserable again. I would start a new eating regime or exercise routine, feel better for a short while, and then I would feel even worse. Eventually, I understood this to be a normal reaction. The body adjusts to the new stimulus over the course of two or three weeks, and you return to the way you felt previously—or even worse.

The reason for this is that adrenal fatigue cannot be improved simply by adding to what you are already doing. You might think of it as trying to fill a cup with a small hole in the bottom. Your energy is continually leaking out and can never be fully replenished, even if you use a gallon bucket to fill it. You can never completely cure the problem just by adding more energy because it is not about more input—it is about fixing the leak. The reason your body feels extraordinarily fatigued is that if it expends more energy than it can produce, then you are in an energy deficit. Over time the deficit increases, until it affects the way you live.

As I have discussed, most of us start this process because an event (large or small) breaches our metabolic threshold and alters the way our body compensates. For me, my event was childbirth. For others, it may be increased stress, a traumatic event, or an illness. For adrenal fatigue patients, these triggers create a vacuum of energy the body cannot seem to replace on its own. It has created the hole in the proverbial cup – an energy deficit that increases over time.

This is one reason family and friends become skeptical of worsening problems. At first, the symptoms do not seem that severe. It is easy to assume the person is simply overdoing it, or is perhaps taking on too much; they are stressed and tired as a result. Since many adrenal fatigue patients work hard to push themselves to perform at an adequate level, they do not even consider that it is a body chemistry problem. In order to replenish what your body is craving, you must eat a healthy, nutritionally balanced diet and include nutritional supplements.

Supplements

Supplements are a vital component for sufferers of adrenal fatigue syndrome. This is because your body is not getting essential nutritional elements via your regular diet. Thus, your body is put into a negative nutritional position that works against your goal of feeling better. While there is a wide range of supplementation available, there are a few that offer particularly significant benefits to anyone suffering from adrenal fatigue.

Calcium – This mineral helps with many cellular functions and with the building of strong bones. It also helps provide energy to muscles. Without enough calcium, the body leaches its calcium reserves; causing bone loss over time. Adding calcium supplements will allow your body to function better and speed your recovery. Low calcium levels can also cause muscle aches, cramps, and pains. These are common maladies among adrenal fatigue sufferers. Calcium also assists with heart regulation. Some adrenal fatigue patients can experience a racing heart or a fluttering sensation. These can be due, in part, to low calcium. Calcium also assists with the transmission of messages throughout the nervous system—again, lacking calcium can cause problems with the nerves, and this can be experienced as pain. Good calcium levels also help to maintain enzyme levels.

Magnesium – This mineral works together with calcium and is vital to maintain a good chemical balance in your body. Magnesium is an important component in the process of energy production and is involved with the reactions of over 300 enzymes. Calcium helps muscles by allowing them to contract more efficiently, whereas magnesium helps them to relax. When the two minerals team up, magnesium helps maintain the balance of calcium within individual cells. Magnesium also assists in regulating hormones. I take a supplement called CalMag™, which combines calcium and magnesium in a proper ratio.

Vitamin C – This vitamin is essential for the creation and maintenance of collagen within the body and is vital for tissue repair. It strengthens blood vessels and is an antioxidant. Vitamin C also allows the body to utilize carbohydrates and to synthesize fats and proteins. Collagen is the most plentiful tissue in the body and functions as connective tissue. This includes cartilage, tendons, and ligaments. Vitamin C also plays a role in the production of antibodies, which stave off infections and help you heal quickly. Adrenal fatigue patients often claim they catch every little cold or sniffle that comes along. In many cases, this is true because their immune system may be compromised by a lack of vitamin C. It is important to know that vitamin C does not stay in the body long, so frequent doses may be necessary.

B Complex Vitamins – The body needs several B vitamins on a regular basis. The following list offers the scientific names of these vitamins as they are sometimes used on supplement labels: thiamine (B1), riboflavin (B2), niacin (B3), pantothenic acid (B5), pyridoxine (B6), biotin (B7), folic acid or folate (B9), cobalamin (B12).

These vitamins as a group are known as B complex vitamins. It is widely known that these vitamins affect numerous systems within the body.

• Vitamin B1 (thiamin) and vitamin B2 (riboflavin) assist in the production of energy and affect enzymes that influence the muscles, nerves, and heart.

• Vitamin B3 (niacin) assists cells and also helps to maintain the health of the skin, nervous system, and digestive system.

• Vitamin B5 (pantothenic acid) allows the body to grow and develop normally.

• Vitamin B6 (pyridoxine) helps to break down protein and maintain the health of red blood cells, the nervous system, and parts of the immune system.

• Vitamin B7 (biotin) also assists in the breakdown of protein as well as carbohydrates and helps the body to make various hormones.

• Vitamin B9 (folic acid) helps the cells in the body to make and maintain DNA and is important in the production of red blood cells. B9 slows the aging of cells.

• Vitamin B12 (cobalamin) assists with growth and development. It also plays a role in producing blood cells, in determining how the body uses folic acid and carbohydrates, and in the functioning of the nervous system.

Deficiency of certain B vitamins can cause anemia, fatigue, loss of appetite, abdominal pain, depression, numbness and tingling in the arms and legs, muscle cramps, respiratory infections, hair loss, and eczema. Many of these same symptoms are noted by adrenal fatigue sufferers, and this highlights the importance of taking adequate amounts of these vitamins.

Digestive Enzymes – Because the bodies of adrenal fatigue patients are out of balance, we may not produce enough digestive enzymes to help us fully utilize the nutrients in our food. For this reason, it is wise to take a high-quality digestive enzyme prior to each meal. This will help break down the food faster and will allow you to get more nutritional benefit. HCL, or hydrochloric acid, is a digestive aid which can assist in the breakdown of protein. Bear in mind, this is not the industrial HCL you may be familiar with—the one used as drain cleaner. The body naturally produces this substance in its stomach acid to break down meats and complex proteins. HCL is available in capsule form at your health food store. Taking too much HCL can cause heartburn. If this happens, just cut back on the dosage and the issue will disappear.

Adrenal Supplementation – My preferred supplements, Cytozyme AD™ and BioImmunozyme Forte™, are from the professional line of Biotics Research Corporation. These are obtained through a licensed healthcare practitioner. Cytozyme AD™ is a formula of specific glandulars and neonatal bovine adrenals created for symptoms of chronic fatigue and lowered resistance, and for adrenal support. BioImmunozyme Forte™ is a broad spectrum of multiple vitamins, co-factors, minerals, and enzymes for support of the immune system.

I also recommend Immunocal™, which is an all-natural dietary supplement in the form of an undenatured whey protein isolate. Immunocal™ is listed in the Physician's Desk Reference (PDR), and its purpose is to naturally boost glutathione levels. This substance delivers cysteine to human cells, which, in turn, helps the immune system to perform at optimal levels. I have used several homeopathic remedies by King Bio. I prefer this line because King Bio products do not contain any additives, which often increase my sensitivity.

A Final Note on Supplements

To determine your specific needs for nutritional supplementation and enzymes, I recommend you find a qualified practitioner trained in nutritional therapy and enzyme therapy. The aforementioned supplements (and many more) may help you, but introduce them slowly, one at a time, so you are able to tell which supplements help you the most. If you introduce too many, you will not know which ones have what impact. You will also want to track the results in your journal, so you have a record to examine should your condition change.

As you are tracking these changes in your body, do not implement any extreme diets. When I began my juice-only diet to cleanse my system, I also decided to sit in a steam tent while I listened to a meditation CD and chanted along with the monks, "I am a mountain. I am strong."

Why was I doing this? *I was convinced these rituals and affirmations were surely going to fix me!* This was a serious error. I needed all my energy reserves, and I was steaming them out of my body and replacing them with only juice!

Picture an already depressed and fragile person dragging her body around, climbing in and out of a steam tent, and juicing every veggie in sight! Drastic measures can lead to drastic setbacks. Each time I crawled into the steam tent, my heart would race out of control. I felt sick and faint, and I was concerned I might have a stroke.

Other examples of extreme diets include any that are too restrictive, including low/no fat and vegetarian diets. It can be difficult for a vegetarian to recover from adrenal fatigue because their diet, by definition, excludes many of the vital nutrients the body requires. You need a well-balanced, organic diet to give your body a starting point. By plunging into an extreme diet, you may break through your metabolic threshold and skew the results of your "guess and test" process. You also should strive to have calm, relaxed meals and never eat too quickly.

There will be times when you take a substance, such as medication, that is supposed to benefit you, but end up feeling worse. This is due to the fact that anything you take alters your blood chemistry. It seems the body becomes so accustomed to an "out-of-balance" state that when there is the sudden introduction of medication or vitamins, even those that may be needed, it can send the body into overload or cross the metabolic threshold. Again, introduce supplementation slowly and over time. Work up to a regular dosage, rather than taking a full dose initially.

Sleep

As a person suffering from adrenal fatigue, you have probably had many people tell you to get more sleep. While common sense would say more rest would help you feel better, it is not that simple. I have lain in bed, countless nights, knowing I needed to sleep. I felt wiped-out, and yet

I could not sleep a wink. Insomnia is a frequent problem with adrenal fatigue, and sleep deprivation can intensify the symptoms and lead to depression.

I knew that when I went to bed at night, I would be lying awake mentally repeating the entire day, and this would exhaust me. Many evenings I would cry, telling my husband and mother that I did not want to go to sleep because I dreaded another day that would be just the same as the previous day. This lack of sleep can lead from mild to deep depression in some people and enhances the medical community's viewpoint that a person with these symptoms is just depressed. Even people who do not have adrenal fatigue have probably experienced bouts of sleep deprivation and understand how detrimental it can be. New parents often experience this during the first weeks or months after they bring their baby home. They walk through their life as zombies just hoping and wishing for a good night's sleep. It affects your ability to reason, operate a vehicle, and just get through the day. Now imagine being in that state for months, or even years.

Like me, many adrenal fatigue sufferers are driven, motivated people. It is difficult for them to accept this condition. They cannot power over it or through it, so it will become debilitating if they do not take care of themselves.

Exercise and Your Environment

Instilled in us is the belief that exercising is important and will give us more energy. Under normal circumstances, this is true. However, for adrenal fatigue sufferers, their systems are not in a "normal" state. Exercise can deplete your body's reserves because, to begin with, you have almost no energy reserves. This does not mean you should become a couch potato. Gentle walking or other forms of light exercise are still desirable, as long as you do not overexert yourself. As you recover, you can add other exercise to your daily routine, but not until the body has had time to restore its chemical balance.

Some beneficial exercises include those involving deep breathing, or those with slow, deliberate movements such as yoga or tai chi. The goal is to reach a calm, relaxed state rather than a sweaty frenzy.

Although you may put exercise on hiatus for a few months while you begin your recovery, you can pay attention to your living environment and make sure it is as healthy as possible. Few people think about the number and types of chemicals they use around their homes. Many cleaners and solvents for home use contain toxins or fumes that can easily breach your metabolic threshold. By replacing these with organic cleaners (available at most major retailers), you can eliminate this possibility.

Problems can also come from household or lawn pesticides, which are extremely toxic. We may not think of mosquito spray or ant killer as pesticides, but they are. Common fertilizers and products used in lawn and garden care can also be toxic and should be avoided entirely. Here again, there are organic alternatives to almost every major chemical used in landscaping or to eliminate pests.

If you live in a major metropolitan area, you may benefit from an air purifier. At certain times of the year, smog and air pollutants can be overwhelming. If your body is weak, you may be more strongly affected than normal. This is especially true if you take walks or if you exercise outdoors. You may wish to limit your outdoor activities during these times and become more aware of the air quality.

New construction is also a source of toxic air. Everything from new paint to new granite countertops can give off fumes or emit substances such as radon into the air. You will want to ventilate the air in a new or remodeled home, so these toxins can be circulated out of the environment.

It may be surprising that something as innocent as washing your hair can be a source of toxins. Many shampoos, soaps, make-up products, deodorants, and perfumes contain chemicals that could cause a reaction. Removing these sources of chemicals from your environment will help you recover faster and improve you overall health.

There was a time, during my most dismal days, that I was convinced there must be something in our home that was contributing to my problems. I hired a feng shui consultant to assess my home, because I was grasping for any help I could get. I looked forward to hearing her observations regarding the energy in my home. Since my personal energy was nonexistent, I was certain that there must be some area of my house that was out of balance. She traveled two hours to get to my home, and after she had completed her walk-through of the house, she informed me I needed to move certain items to different locations throughout the house, and I needed to buy other important elements.

It is wonderful that my husband loves me. We soon had three fountains properly placed, per feng shui guidelines, and some jingly charms hanging everywhere. I even mounted a mirror behind my stove-top, because she declared it was an area that had a definite problem with energy. In fact, it was a problem as it turned out, because it required a lot of my energy just to keep the mirror clean! All this may have been a shot in the dark, but looking back, it was also a sign that I never gave up hope, even if that hope were a long shot.

Each day is a new canvas to paint upon. Make sure your picture is full of life and happiness, and at the end of the day you don't look at it and wish you had painted something different.

- Author Unknown

Chapter 8

Do I Have to be Special?

Knowing yourself is the beginning of all wisdom.

- Aristotle

The emphatic answer is: "Yes, you will be special." Many people with adrenal fatigue become frustrated because the only way to discover the triggers for their symptoms requires a good amount of "guess and test." This may be tedious. Even when you think you have it down, something will occasionally blindside you and leave you drained. The psychological aspects of this syndrome are, by far, the most dangerous, because you could easily become convinced there is no hope or that the continuing pursuit of an answer is far too difficult. It is vital to pay attention to your mental, emotional, and spiritual health while you work through the process of recovery.

The body is a perfect and complex system, and if it has a shortfall it might be the inability to distinguish life's normal stress from life-threatening stress. The body is unable to determine the difference, which is what sends our systems into overdrive. The body reacts to stress regardless of the source of the stress—it does not make any difference if it is from money problems or from being a prisoner-of-war. The body treats them all the same.

Adrenal fatigue syndrome is the body at war. It is fighting to save your life (a battle of day-to-day life), and you are living in the battle zone. When you think of it this way, you know you must be emotionally strong to overcome. This is not just some bump on the knee; it is war.

It is difficult for sufferers to eliminate negative thought processes. As they navigate through the medical mine field, there is a great deal of negativity to deal with in the traditional medical community, as well as with those who are skeptical. In my case, much of that negativity was associated with guilt. I felt guilty because I knew I was not the wife I wanted to be, or because I could not be the perfect mother for my children. I felt guilty when I could not work, or when I could not get off the couch for days. I mentally beat myself up repeatedly, as many adrenal fatigue patients do.

It is vital to understand how negativity affects your behavior and emotions. Replaying negative thoughts will make recovery that much more difficult because the body will energize what we recognize. Since the body cannot distinguish one type of stress from another, if we spend our days focusing on negative and contentious situations, there is a consequence. Our bodies will respond by sending out the adrenaline army and perpetuating the cycle. In some cases, adrenal patients will develop behaviors consistent with an obsessive-compulsive disorder (OCD), as I did with my obsession about cleaning and order. Others may develop a fear of driving or flying. I experienced this as well. The fear can be so real that it will cause a physical reaction.

Previously, I talked about the inability to relax when I would lie down at night. My mind would replay, as if on an endless video loop, each and every detail of my day. There were no good days to recall, which made it horrible to relive. I could not let go. Learning techniques for overcoming negative thought patterns will help you break this cycle. One technique that worked for me was repeating the word "cancel" each time a negative thought came to mind. I visualized a process much like hitting the "delete" button on the computer. Each time the thought would appear, I would vigorously repeat "cancel" to delete it. I also decided to wear a bracelet with an angel on it, and each time I experienced fear or had a negative thought, I would rub the angel. Needless to say, I almost rubbed that little angel's wings off!

The perspective we bring to each day makes a difference in the way we approach challenges—and with this syndrome, the challenges are many! If you can reduce your negative thoughts, there is hope for recovery,

You can quickly be swallowed by a whirlpool of negativity. In order to have a defense, you must identify when you are replaying an event or a thought. As a negative thought enters your mind, you can willfully convert it to a positive. For example, if the repetitive thought is, "I am not a good mother, I am not a good mother," you can force yourself to concentrate on the sweet gestures your children say and do. Focusing on good is an exercise in guided imagery. Just as the body does not distinguish between different types of stress, the mind considers positive thoughts as if the positive events are actually happening. Focusing on positive events and ideas will alter the body's functions and chemistry. What you recognize, you energize, and as these positive ideas gain energy they will manifest in your life.

Though it may seem hard right now, it is very important that gratitude become your new attitude. Gratitude is a powerful emotion. If you are able to feel grateful for something—anything—this will help you to combat the dark cloud that seems to have descended.

For many, including me, it helps to pray. Your religious leaning is not as relevant as the fact that you have a belief system that allows you to draw upon the strength of a higher power. Prayer can be a source of help. Make no mistake, God and I had a tumultuous relationship while I was recovering. There were times I wished for the strength to throw stones at heaven for making me suffer while clinging to the belief that there is a higher power than me to help me through it.

On Sundays, I would kneel at the church altar and pray. I would beg God to heal me and allow me to escape from this hell. I can still remember how my hands were shaking, and I even felt as if my hair were shaking, as I prayed at the altar in front of hundreds of people. I did not care. I was desperate. I would repeat the phrase daily, "God has a plan, and His plan is good," even though many days I had grave doubts. My religious beliefs are, and continue to be, a source of strength. You may have the same experience, and I encourage you to lean on your belief system during your recovery.

One of the toughest struggles I had was dealing with unintentional toxic people in my life. It is true, you cannot always choose relationships. There may be a few family members and friends in your life that can cause tremendous stress and deplete your energy. It is valuable to write in your journal when stressful situations occur, even when you do not wish to write about uncomfortable subjects. You can always burn those pages later once you understand the effect specific relationships have on your life. Still, many patients are hesitant to acknowledge that it is someone close to them causing the stress, because it is very difficult to deal with the guilt.

In my experience, there were a few family members/friends that seemed capable of sucking the life out of me in just a few minutes and one in particular. It was not entirely possible to avoid this person, and I did not want to cause a rift. Since I could not avoid the situation, I learned to spend short amounts of time with this person and to take frequent breaks to decompress.

Even at seemingly benign activities, such as my children's sports events or at church, there were individuals who could overwhelm me on occasion. I was accustomed to being in control, so the concept of another personality overwhelming me was foreign at first. As I took note of my feelings after being around these individuals, I became aware that this was actually happening. Journaling gave me the clues to recognize these people and manage my time with them, before they drained my vitality.

Some adrenal patients become intuitive, or perhaps others are born with intuitiveness. They can feel emotions from people that others may not notice. I have, over the years, been amazed at my insight into certain individuals or situations that I instantly recognized correctly with almost no background information. You must follow this feeling and learn to not second guess your initial impressions. This is a gift that will enable you to avoid many difficult situations.

The following is my personality classification system for how you can recognize some of the signals and signs of various types of individuals that can drain your energy. Each of these types can exist in one person or someone may be a combination of them.

Just being aware of what is happening with the people around you gives you an advantage and opportunity to reduce your stress before it occurs. Many of these traits are incorporated into the personalities of people that you love and they love you. Eventually, the alert friends and family members will begin to notice and make a strong effort to not incorporate negativity, conflict and stress into your relationships. Others are very covert in their methods and have no intentions of changing. Remember that you may have helped develop these different relationships during a time when you were well and could endure. When you are in more vulnerable state with adrenal fatigue, you may simply be unable to spare the energy needed to maintain the previous dynamics of the relationships.

Master Manipulator

There are people who are master manipulators. It is not uncommon for you to say "yes" to their requests, and then 10 minutes later wonder, "What just happened?" One of the tricks used by this personality type is to find and push your buttons. They can have a way of eroding your belief systems and self-esteem, and they can easily convince you that their priorities are the most important.

One of my hot buttons is my children. Even the subtle hint that my children were missing out by their lack of participation in *another* activity was a negative, yet provided a fool-proof way for someone to squeeze a "yes" out of me, even when I had been absolutely committed to saying, "NO." A friend once convinced me, via guilt of course, that I must have my kids join her kids' swim team. This was the summer when I was on bed rest, but because I believed I *must* do certain things to be considered a good mother, I signed them up. I knew I could not physically handle the schedule or participate in volunteering. This could be chalked up on the "board of good intentions", and as it turned out, I did not have the capability to complete the mission. I felt guilty, my kids were disappointed, and my friend must have wondered what in the world was wrong with me.

Adrenal fatigue sufferers, by their very nature, have an enormous amount of guilt. This sets up them up as easy pickings for the manipulator. The best defense with this type of person is the quick "no and go." Say no and disappear quickly—then remain unreachable so they cannot convince you to change your mind. Screen your calls or if necessary, send an email saying you have gone to Tahiti for a month—whatever it takes. You are not responsible for making someone else feel pleased about themselves, or for giving them what they want. You are only responsible for you; let go of any guilt associated with being "unavailable or unable."

The Self-Involved

Everyone has a friend or family member that is self-involved. They will call and want to meet for lunch, or they want to spend time with you, just so they can tell you *all* about their lives. There are many times when they will show little or no interest in what is going on with you, and if you bring up anything about your life, they will reply with a quick "UhHuh." Then, they immediately dismiss your part of the conversation and change the topic back to themselves. Because they are rather narcissistic and are focused on their own wants, needs, and desires, you may feel let down and unfulfilled after you have spent time with this person. They may require so much of your focus that your energy is drained.

These individuals are not as easy to hide from, as they are also manipulative. Their power comes from having an audience and from telling their story, so they will probably know your habits and will easily track you down. If they perceive your non-attentiveness as ditching them intentionally, they may create a rumor and then spread it. It is a form of entertainment for them designed to bring your attention back to them.

The best defense for this type of person is distance. The more you are unavailable to listen to them, the more likely they will find someone else to listen to their tales.

The Killjoy

This personality will look at a beautiful sunset and do nothing but gripe about the mosquitoes. They will attend a graduation ceremony and make the prediction that the graduate will probably spend the next few years unemployed or stuck in a job they can't stand with coworkers they hate. Regardless of the situation, they will zero in on the negative and add emphasis to it. Pretty much anything you say to them will bring a litany of warnings and predictions of doom.

You would think a killjoy personality would find a kindred spirit in an adrenal fatigue patient since they frequently have a similar depressing and negative outlook on life, but this is not the case. As you struggle to pull yourself out from under the dark cloud, the killjoys are experts at pointing out repeatedly how likely you are to fall-short or fail. When you begin to improve, your new and brighter outlook can be fragile. A mere five minutes with this type of person can send you right back into the fatigue you so want to escape.

This is definitely one personality type you may not be able to spend much time around, even after you recover. If they continue to be negative and pessimistic, the only cure is distance. The danger of falling back into that mindset may always be with you.

Judge-and-Jury

A close cousin to the Killjoy is the Judge-and-Jury personality. If you enjoy something, they find flaws. If you have a new accomplishment, the Judge-and-Jury will go on and on about what a poor idea it was and then will counter with what they would have said or done in that situation. Any opinion, other than theirs, is insignificant, and they play on your guilt. They know what qualities (in their own minds) the best spouse, mother, or friend are comprised of, and they may even point out every area where you fall short of their ideal.

It is paramount to note that this person's standards are his or hers alone. You are not required to live up to anyone else's ideal. It can be easy to adopt someone else's criteria, especially if they are a family member. In-laws, siblings, and parents could inadvertently lead the charge to make you feel you do not measure up. Nothing can be further from the truth; the only expectations you should focus on are getting through each day and protecting your recovery.

The Judge-and-Jury personalities can be so overbearing that you must remove yourself from their presence. They will stall your efforts to improve. They do not dream of what *can* be, or believe that people can change. They will not be encouraging and will be the most surprised when you recover. Then they may suggest you have rallied enough and you will not make any more progress.

An insightful point to make is that many adrenal sufferers (me included) *are* this type of person, but not in the respect that we have high expectations for others. Rather, we have high expectations for ourselves. My vision of the ideal "perfect wife" or the "perfect mother" was mine alone. It was not a standard someone else set for me. It was one I created, and then one I used to beat myself up!

Insidious Insincerity

Many people have acquaintances, friends, or extended family members who are insincere. They humor you, but still make you feel small. They refuse to join in your excitement about anything and seem to be around to ensure you never get the spotlight. They give only lip service to being concerned about any aspect of your life.

This relationship is hollow. Deep down, you know that if you needed this person, he or she will not be available. It is as if they would prefer you fail so they can stand back and gloat.

The Seat of Disrespect

Disrespect has different meanings to different people. For the purposes of this discussion, "disrespect" refers to the type of person who will blurt out awkward or irreverent comments. They are also divisive with their inappropriate actions at the worst, most embarrassing, or random times. They are grownup schoolyard bullies. Frequently, they are someone you have confided in, or perhaps known since your childhood such as a close family friend or even a family member. Since they know so much about your life, they attempt to use your failures or weak moments against you. They may be a parent or a sibling who professes to love you, but they stick their nose into every aspect of your life—whether it belongs there or not.

The problem with these individuals is they have no sense of boundaries or imperative territory. They are not respecters of your feelings, your privacy, or any aspect of your life. Regardless of the situation, you can never trust what they will do or say. This puts you on "highest alert" and causes tremendous stress, even if nothing occurs. It is perpetually on your mind that eventually these people could strike, and a disaster may ensue. The stress from anticipation is just as acute as an actual stressful event.

With this type of person, you have to refuse to give in to that stress. While you can insist they back off, constant confrontation will dissipate your energy. A hiatus from this person may be in order.

The Never Ending Vacuum

There are people in this world you cannot please no matter what you do. I like to picture them as giant vacuums sucking the life out of people. They are often referred to as "energy vampires" because they can never get enough; you can never do, say, or be enough to please them. These people rarely take responsibility for anything in their lives and are endlessly needy. They usually will take others for granted, and they have unrealistic expectations that no one, including themselves, could fulfill. They want every event in life to be a Hallmark moment. Sorry, that is not real life.

These toxic personalities have several commonalities, including the fact that most of them do not feel as if they are doing anything wrong. In fact, they may believe they are helping you, either by refusing to talk about your problems or by dwelling on your shortfalls. Unfortunately, the more they get away with their toxic behavior, the more they engage in it. Doubtlessly, they realize some reward from their actions. Perhaps, they feel superior, or more intelligent, or any of hundreds of emotions.

It can be a revelation, because once you realize that you are the least of their concerns, you can let go of the guilt for limiting contact with them. Unhitching yourself from the guilt can allow you to move forward.

If I have discovered anything, it is that life is too short to allow others to rob you of the vital energy you need to have a fulfilling life. Relationships, by nature, induce stress, and each person will have a different reality about the world. Slow down and allow peace to enter your mind as an important first step toward what you really want—*your life back.*

Perseverance is failing nineteen times and succeeding the twentieth.

- Julie Andrews

Chapter 9

Living Again

Don't limit yourself. Many people limit themselves to what they think they can do. You can go as far as your mind lets you. What you believe, remember, you can achieve.

- Mary Kay Ash

The Daisy symbolizes childlike joy and playfulness and is my symbol of recovery.

There were times during my recovery that I could not believe my life would ever be "normal" again. This began during my initial struggle with adrenal fatigue syndrome, even when I did not know what was wrong with me. There is not an actual state of "normal," and what I had assumed to be my picture of normal never existed. Now, I know there was a better life waiting for me; I just had to embrace it. I have gone from being an enthusiastic young wife and mother, to floundering in a pit of despair, to recovery and maintenance. If I accomplish nothing else from writing this book, I want you realize there *is* hope. You can (and will) learn to live with and control this syndrome. Along the way, you will also discover more about yourself than you ever suspected.

The journey of personal growth begins with an awareness of both the psychological and the physical aspects of adrenal fatigue. It is only once you recognize the depth and breadth of the problem that you can accept it. Acceptance is a bitter pill to swallow; it certainly was for me. I had to admit I was not perfect. I was not a superwoman, and no matter how hard I strived to fake it, there was no hiding from reality. No matter how hard I tried or how much I wished to be okay, I was not. It was not until I accepted that I had to focus on my health that I started to witness changes for the better.

It has been difficult to put myself first. I wanted to be a rock, a solid foundation, for everyone in my life, but I could not if my health were destroyed. I had to accept that it was in everyone's best interest for me to find out what was wrong. Even now, I sometimes slip back into the habit of putting everyone and everything else first. Now I recognize this tendency and protect myself from allowing my energy to be drained. No one will make your health a priority if you do not, and even if you are alone, it is up to you to choose to change.

One question I grappled with throughout my recovery was, "Why? Why did this happen to me? What did I ever do to deserve this?" The answer was that I did not do anything, but by overcoming I have become a stronger person. I have gained a greater understanding of myself and those around me. Now, I can help others. I can say I legitimately care about what people feel, and I want to open more of my experiences and my life to others. My journey has helped me to open my heart to real caring – not a preconceived nor contrived caring!

When I was lying in my bed suffering and hoping the mattress would swallow me, if someone had suggested that I would someday write a book, I would have gathered my last bit of strength to laugh in their face! You are now reading my words, and they are proof that an adrenal fatigue sufferer can overcome and achieve miraculous outcomes. I am not glossing over the fact that the journey was bleak and tedious, but it was worth every second of heartache and sorrow to get back to being *me*—the real *me* that I was meant to be. For the first time in years, I feel as if I am finally back and participating fully in my life. I am not wandering about as a dispassionate and lethargic zombie, like a prisoner of war waiting to be rescued.

Of course, the benefits of recovery are numerous and have affected every area of my life. First and foremost, I just feel better. My days now include cooking for my family, and I love to cook. Before, the nausea and fatigue made me want to toss my cookies every time I attempted to make a meal. Now, I can do my girls' hair and make it to work—all before 9:00 a.m. I am so proud that when I handle a problem, I am no longer a tiger or dictator. On weekends, my family can now enjoy each other without me ruining a joyous time because I am so tired I have to cancel.

I now can make my children feel special. I bake cookies with them, and I go outside with my girls to do something as simple as fly a kite! I created a list of activities we can do together. The list includes experiences that are childlike, inexpensive and spontaneous – yet rich in emotion and caring. Each week I check off one.

Because I have learned so much about myself on this incredible journey, I want to hear people's thoughts and ideas. We are all different, and we all have different realities. I plan to continue embracing the unassuming, childlike joys that were stolen from me. So now, when I sway on a tire swing or walk through the woods and look for wild flowers, I find myself peering at life as if through the eyes of my children—it is wondrous and mystical.

Before my recovery, I would only observe the unsatisfactory and disappointing parts of my life, because I felt I was fighting a battle against death, and even though I was alone in this belief, my mind allowed this idea to continue to creep toward me. Again and again, I was convinced that I must be dying. I could barely drag myself to the table and fake my way through dinner; I just wanted it to be finished and escape to the cover of my bedroom. I am now active each day. I make my bed each morning knowing I will not be seeing the sheets again until bedtime.

My relationships have grown stronger, too. I now have an even stronger bond with my husband and my mother, both of whom were with me every step of the way. I love my mother so much; she never gave up and continually talked with me and always took my calls, even if they were in the middle of the night. I was afraid, and I needed to talk. I desperately needed reassurance, and she provided that. I will do anything that improves her life and will be on call for her at a second's notice because I can never repay the support, love, and patience she has shown.

My husband and I are in our second decade of marriage, and I feel peace each day knowing that no matter what, everything will be okay. I have my faith to guide me. We have survived and thrived in love.

My children are now benefiting from a mother who is really there and is fully engaged in their upbringing. The transformation from a hollowed soul of a person to a productive, happy person changed not only my life, but the lives of all those around me. I remember the day my husband came home from the office, and I was on the telephone, still working. He was amazed by my energy, but he was annoyed by my eagerness to make up for lost time. We proceeded to talk and then have a small argument about my not sitting down with the family for dinner. I had prepared the dinner, but I just had not made it to the table. I was too busy. My daughter, Olivia, ran into the kitchen and cried, "Daddy, Mommy feels better, and we have her back. She just feels happy." Those were the wise words of an 8-year-old little girl, and they made me feel great. My little Olivia can now plan an enjoyable day with me or wake me in the night and not feel guilty because I am too tired or sick.

I was engrossed in my planning and achieving mode while my husband was still looking at me as being bedridden. The people in your life will adjust to your recovery, but they may require time. I was overdoing things as I recovered, but I just wanted to gather up my life and run around with it after spending so much time merely existing.

My oldest daughter, Elaina, has a nurturing, motherly side. It steadily developed by teaching her little sister how to ride a bike or by helping her learn to tie her shoes. She did these as expressions of love, because her Mommy was too tired. Now, she now can feel confident that I am there to do those perhaps small, yet momentous, activities that she so gracefully accomplished and did for me while I was too tired.

We are planning future birthday parties for my girls. The most celebrated gift is that now a celebration could span an entire day instead of 60 minutes (or less) because I might need to fall back into bed. My children can relive their childhood with me, such as drawing on the sidewalk with chalk or having summer water fights. While we cannot erase my hollow years, we can enjoy the present and fully intend to do so.

People wafting in and out of my life are now less likely to affect me negatively, because I choose those with whom I share my time. I have given myself permission to maintain my distance from people who are a negative drain. I find that my "nega-vibe" radar alerts me very quickly to these situations, and I follow my instincts. This starts with my social circle and trickles all the way down to the people I hire or with whom I do business.

It is not the number of friends you have on your Facebook account; it is the quality of friends with whom you share your life. Recently, I attended a lawn party and was talking with a group. There was a lady who proceeded to share all of her negative views and lash out about others' conversations. I felt anxiety and an escalated, heightened state of alarm. Her negativity was like a cloud of dye from an octopus; once it is expelled into the ocean, soon all the water in that area is polluted. I looked around at everyone's faces and body language, and guess what? Their lips were pierced, and their eyes were squinted. Some had their hands clenched; others looked down or elsewhere, as if trying to escape the situation and join in the activities of others.

I quietly stood up and strolled away from the group. I knew my best course of action was removal. I could not remove her, nor do I have that right. It is my problem, so I picked myself up and proceeded on my recovered way. These choices make me happy because I know they are in my own best interest, and in the best interest of everyone involved in my recovery. Now, I am strong enough to choose, and you will be too.

The Last First Step

I have taken a thousand first-steps on my long road to recovery. Many of my steps were counterproductive. When I started on my final journey to recovery, I had no inkling that the next step I would take would be my last *first step*. I had undertaken so many endeavors; I looked for something, anything that would help me. My learning curve was long and slow, but I hope that through reading this book, yours will be much shorter.

Today, I have a profound sense of gratitude for everything I have experienced. That may sound strange to hear because the road has been so hard and long, but my journey is an example for the millions of people who do, and will, suffer from this syndrome. My joy comes from knowing the struggle was worthwhile and from understanding I can help those who are just starting out or struggling through their own journey.

If there is anything I can leave with you, it is my wish for you to find your joy. Finding your joy can bring about a miracle each day, because joy makes our small delights bigger. It may be a flicker at first, like a lone candle in a moonless night, but over time you can nurture that flame into a heartfelt glow that cannot be extinguished.

I will be on your side during your journey because this is real. I believe you. It is not all in your mind. Do not feel lonely—I am here. I want to give you what I wish I would have had: a friend who already walked in these shoes and came back to life. You have my heartfelt hope and belief that you will take that last first-step and grasp the life that awaits you.

What seems to us as bitter trials are often blessings in disguise.

- Oscar Wilde

Adrenal Fatigue Symptom Matrix

			Adrenal Fatigue	Chronic Fatigue	Fibro-myalgia
Mind	Anxieties	General Anxiety	X	X	X
		Fearfulness	X		
		Anxiety-related rapid breathing		X	
		Anxiety-related trouble breathing			X
		Shallow breathing	X		X
		Panic attacks	X	X	X
	Mood & Emotion	Intuitiveness	X		
		Impatience	X		
		Quick to anger	X		
		Irritability	X	X	X
		Depression	X	X	X
		Excessive com-pulsive	X		
		Inability to cope	X	X	X
		Diminished sex drive	X	X	X
	Cognitive	Brain fog	X	X	X
		Loss of concen-tration	X	X	X
		Memory loss	X	X	X

			Adrenal Fatigue	Chronic Fatigue	Fibro-myalgia
Body	Sensitivities	Allergies	X	X	
		Hyper sensitivities			X
		Sensitivity to cold	X		
		Temperature sensitivity			X
		Sensitivity to light	X	X	X
	Aches & Pains	Arthritis-like symptoms	X	X	X
		Headaches	X	X	X
		Muscle aches	X	X	X
		General pain	X	X	X
		Exercise intolerance	X	X	X
	Hair	Thin, straw-like hair	X		
		Dry, course, thinning hair		X	
		Temporary hair loss			X

			Adrenal Fatigue	Chronic Fatigue	Fibro-myalgia
Body	Heart & Circulatory System	Heart palpitations	X	X	X
		Rapid heartbeat	X	X	
		Low blood pressure	X	X	X
		Tightness in chest	X		
		Chest pain	X	X	X
		Lightheadedness	X	X	X
		Dizziness	X	X	X
		Numbness/Tingling in hands and feet		X	X
	Digestive	Gastrointestinal problems			X
		Irregularity	X		
		Poor digestion and absorption	X	X	X
		Sweet or salty cravings	X		
		Sugar or carb cravings		X	
		General food cravings			X
		Weight loss or gain	X	X	X
		Loss of appetite	X	X	X
		Nausea	X	X	X

			Adrenal Fatigue	Chronic Fatigue	Fibro-myalgia
Body	Illness	Sore throat	X	X	X
		Fever	X	X	X
		Swollen lymph nodes	X		
		Frequent Influ-enza	X		
		Flu-like feelings		X	
		Tender lymph nodes		X	X
		Low blood sugar	X	X	X
		Low adrenal func-tion	X	X	X
		Low immune function	X	X	X
		Chronic cough	X	X	X
	Reproductive	Menopause or related symptoms	X	X	X
		PMS	X	X	X
		Painful periods			X
		Painful inter-course		X	
	Bladder	Frequent urination	X		X
		Unable to empty bladder	X	X	
		Urgency			X

			Adrenal Fatigue	Chronic Fatigue	Fibro-myalgia
Body	Sleep	Unrefreshing sleep	X	X	
		Insomnia	X	X	
		Sleeping disorders			X
	Skin & Muscle	Clammy/cold hands and feet		X	
		Sweating	X	X	X
		Itchy, dry, blotchy skin	X		X
		Skin rash		X	
		Restless leg syn-drome	X		X
		Muscle twitching			X
		Weakness	X	X	X
		Severe fatigue	X	X	X
	Jaw & Mouth	Jaw pain	X	X	X
		Jaw clicking	X		
		Facial pain			X
		Dry mouth	X	X	X
		Dental problems	X	X	X

Quick Self-Assessment

The quickest and easiest way to see if you may have adrenal fatigue is a blood pressure test. For this test, you should lie down for a few minutes before taking your blood pressure in this position. Once those numbers are recorded, stand up and then retake your blood pressure immediately.

In a normal person, your blood pressure will rise when you are in a sitting or standing position (as opposed to lying down) because the heart must work against gravity to pump the blood around your body and this requires adrenaline. When a person with adrenal fatigue stands, their blood pressure drops because they can't muster that quick shot of adrenalin. For example, when I would take my blood pressure lying down, it would be 100/50. When I stood, it would be 90/40. Sometimes the drop was larger, sometimes it was smaller, but it did not rise as it normally should have. This is a quick way to test yourself and see if your symptoms may be adrenal related.

Additional Resources

Adrenal Fatigue: The 21st Century Stress Syndrome (2002) by James L. Wilson, foreword by Johnathan V. Wright. Published by Smart Publications.

Chronic Fatigue Syndrome for Dummies (2007) by Susan R. Lisman M.D. and Karla Dougherty. Published by Wiley Publishing, Inc.

The Doctor's Guide To Chronic Fatigue Syndrome: Understanding, Treating, And Living With Cfids (1995) by David S. Bell. Published by Da Capo Press.

Dr. Gerald E. Poesnecker

Dr. Poesnecker was one of the first physicians to write about adrenal fatigue and identify ways to treat the syndrome. His books include:

It's Only Natural (1975)

Adrenal Syndrome (1983)

Chronic Fatigue Unmasked (1993)

It's Only Natural (Revised 4th Edition) (1996)

Chronic Fatigue Unmasked 2000 (1999)

Mastering Your Life (2002)

Glossary

Acute: Sudden or severe. Acute symptoms appear, change, or worsen rapidly.

Adrenal Fatigue Syndrome: A stress-induced condition characterized by a set of common symptoms that indicate decreased function of the adrenal glands. Also known as hypoadrenia, adrenal exhaustion, adrenal insufficiency, adrenal gland fatigue, adrenal chronic fatigue, and non-addisons hypoadrenia.

Adrenal Glands: The adrenal glands are small, thumbprint-sized glands atop your kidneys, consisting of the inner core, called the medulla, and the outer layer, called the cortex.

Adrenaline: A substance secreted by the adrenal gland in response to stress that stimulates autonomic nerve action.

Adrenal Cortex: The outer layer of the adrenal gland that produces many different hormones, including cortisol, aldosterone, pregnenalone, sex hormones (estrogen, progesterone, testosterone), and DHEA.

Adrenal Medulla: The inner core of the adrenal glands. It is responsible for triggering the "fight or flight" response of the sympathetic nervous system to urgent stress. Epinephrine (adrenaline) and norepinephrine are the two main hormones produced here.

Addison's Disease: A complete lack of adrenal function. The most severe form of hypoadrenia.

Aldosterone: Aldosterone is a mineralocorticoid that helps to regulate your blood pressure by maintaining the mineral balance in your cells, including potassium, magnesium, and sodium.

Allergies: An abnormally high sensitivity to certain substances, such as pollens, foods, or microorganisms. Common indications of allergy may include sneezing, itching, and skin rashes.

Antidepressant: Pharmaceutical agents used to treat clinical depression.

Anxiety: Also known as anxiety neurosis or anxiety reaction. A condition that can be caused by both psychological and physiologic factors. It can take two general forms: (1) acute anxiety (panic disorder), marked by repeated occurrences of intense self-limited anxiety lasting usually a few minutes to an hour, or (2) chronic anxiety, characterized by less intense reactions of much longer duration (days, weeks, or months).

Autoimmune Disease: Disorders in which the body mounts a destructive immune response against its own tissues.

Bio-Identical Hormones: Bio-identical hormones are natural (usually plant-based) hormone substances that are nearly identical in structure and chemical composition to the hormones your body produces on its own.

Blood Pressure: The pressure exerted by the blood against the walls of the blood vessels, especially the arteries. It varies with the strength of the heartbeat, the elasticity of the arterial walls, the volume and viscosity of the blood, and a person's health, age, and physical condition.

Blood Sugar: Sugar in the form of glucose in the blood.

Body Chemistry: A term used to describe the interaction of the chemicals produced by and ingested by the body.

Burn Out: Physical or emotional exhaustion, especially as a result of long-term stress or dissipation.

CAM Therapies: Complementary and alternative medicine (CAM) therapies are those outside standard medical therapies that compliment traditional therapies.

Carbohydrates (Complex): Complex carbohydrates are the carbohydrate molecules formed by the chains of three or more single sugar molecules linked together. Long chains of sugar molecules are called starches and they serve as the storage form of energy in plants. It is called a complex carbohydrate because its fiber content remains intact. Vegetables, breads, cereals, legumes, and pasta are good examples.

Carbohydrates (Simple): These are found naturally in foods such as fruits, milk, and milk products. They are also found in processed and refined sugars such as candy, table sugar, syrups, and soft drinks. Simple carbohydrates are broken down quickly by the body to be used as energy.

Cartilage: A tough, elastic, fibrous connective tissue found in various parts of the body, such as the joints and larynx.

Chiropractor: Physician who diagnosis and treats patients based on the concept that the nervous system coordinates all of the body's functions, and that disease results from a lack of normal nerve function. Chiropractic employs manipulation and adjustment of body structures, such as the spinal column, so that pressure on nerves coming from the spinal cord due to displacement (subluxation) of a vertebral body may be relieved.

Chlorine: A common nonmetallic element belonging to the halogens; best known as a heavy yellow irritating toxic gas; used to purify water and as a bleaching agent.

Chronic Fatigue Syndrome: Having severe chronic fatigue of six months or longer duration with other known medical conditions excluded by clinical diagnosis and concurrently have four or more of the following symptoms: substantial impairment in short-term memory or concentration; sore throat; tender lymph nodes; muscle pain; multi-joint pain without swelling or redness; headaches of a new type, pattern or severity; unrefreshing sleep; and post-exertional malaise lasting more than 24 hours. The symptoms must have persisted or recurred during six or more consecutive months of illness and must not have predated the fatigue.

Compounding Pharmacy: A pharmacy that prepares prescriptions designed specifically for individual patients, as they are ordered. Bio-identical hormones can be compounded in unique combinations for an individualized treatment.

Cortisol: A glucocorticoid hormone produced by the adrenal cortex. Cortisol plays a part in the metabolism of carbohydrates, proteins, and fats, as well as interacting with insulin to regulate the rise and fall of glucose (blood sugar) levels in the body. It helps regulate blood pressure and water balance. As one of the body's naturally produced steroids, it also plays a part in controlling inflammation.

Circulatory System: The bodily system consisting of the heart, blood vessels, and blood that circulates blood throughout the body, delivers nutrients and other essential materials to cells, and removes waste products. Also called *cardiovascular system*.

Cushing's Syndrome: Extreme hyperadrenia.

Chronic: Of long duration, denoting a disease of slow progress and long continuance.

Cysteine: An amino acid derived from cystine and found in most proteins.

DHEA (Dehydroepiandrosterone): An androgenic steroid hormone secreted mostly by the adrenal cortex and found in human urine.

Depression: A neurotic or psychotic condition marked by an inability to concentrate, insomnia, and feelings of dejection and guilt.

Detoxify: To reduce or eliminate the buildup of damaging compounds in the body.

Digestive System: The system in the body used to process food and turn it into energy.

Endocrine System: The bodily system that consists of the endocrine glands and functions to regulate body.

Endocrine Disruptors: Chemicals that mimic hormones in your body. These wreak havoc in many different ways.

Energy Vampire: An individual who has a very negative energy that drains the emotions and energy of other people.

Enzymes: Any of numerous proteins or conjugated proteins produced by living organisms and functioning as biochemical catalysts.

Fatigue: Temporary loss of strength and energy.

Fertilizer: Any of a large number of natural and synthetic materials, including manure and nitrogen, phosphorus, and potassium compounds, spread on or worked into soil to increase its capacity to support plant growth.

Fight or Flight: a set of physiological changes, such as increases in heart rate, arterial blood pressure, and blood glucose, initiated by the sympathetic nervous system to mobilize body systems in response to stress.

Fibromyalgia: A chronic disorder characterized by widespread pain, tenderness, and stiffness of muscles and associated connective tissues and generally accompanied by fatigue, headaches, and sleep disturbance and insomnia.

GMOs: A genetically modified organism (GMO) or genetically engineered organism (GEO) is an organism whose genetic material has been altered using genetic engineering techniques.

Glutathione: An antioxidant, protects cells from toxins such as free radicals.

Genetic Engineering: Scientific alteration of the structure of genetic material in a living organism.

Gastrointestinal Complaints: Problems experienced with the digestive system.

Heart Palpitations: An abnormal awareness of the beating of the heart, whether it is too slow, too fast, irregular, or at its normal frequency.

Heavy Metals: A metal with a specific gravity greater than about 5.0, especially one that is poisonous, such as lead.

Herbicides: A chemical substance used to destroy or inhibit the growth of plants, especially weeds.

Homeopathic: A system of therapy based upon the concept that disease can be treated with drugs (in minute doses) considered to be capable of producing the same symptoms in healthy people as the disease itself.

Hormones: Chemical substances that act like messenger molecules in the body.

Hypersensitive: A heightened sensitivity to various stimuli including allergens, smells, light, etc.

Hypothalamic-Pituitary-Adrenal (HPA) Axis: The combined system of neuroendocrine units that in a negative feedback network regulate the adrenal gland's hormonal activities.

Immune Compromised: A condition in which the patient has a higher risk of infection due to a weak immune system.

Influenza: An acute, contagious, infectious disease, caused by any of various viruses and characterized by inflammation of the respiratory tract, fever, and muscular pain.

Insomnia: Inability to sleep even in the absence of external impediments during the period when sleep should normally occur.

Intuition: An internal knowing derived from feelings.

Joint: A junction where two bones meet. Most joints are composed of cartilage, joint space, fibrous capsule, synovium, and ligaments.

Lactose: A sugar comprising one glucose molecule linked to a galactose molecule; occurs only in milk.

Lymph Nodes: Oval-shaped masses of tissue that filter for a fluid called lymph. They are responsible for removing cell waste and ultimately help the body fight off infection. Lymph nodes are scattered throughout the body.

Magnesium: Mineral responsible for many enzymatic reactions and progesterone production. Low magnesium can result in PMS, osteoporosis, and abnormal heart rhythm.

Malaise: A feeling of discomfort, uneasiness, or out-of-sorts feeling, often an indicator of an infection or other disease.

Mineral: Any naturally occurring, inorganic substance, often additionally characterized by an exact crystal structure.

Muscle: Specialized cells in the body that are controlled by the brain and allow motion.

Myalgic Encephalomyelitis: A synonym for chronic fatigue syndrome.

Naturopathy: A method of treating disease using food, exercise, and heat to assist the natural healing process.

Nervous System: The sensory and control apparatus of the body consisting of a network of nerve cells.

OB/GYN: Physician specializing in obstetrics and gynecology.

Obsessive Compulsive Disorder (OCD): A psychological problem that manifests in the compulsion for repetitive acts and extreme order in a person's environment.

Panic Attacks: Debilitating emotional stress/fear induced by an imagined negative event.

Pesticides: A substance or mixture of substances used to kill pests, usually insects.

Phosphates: An inorganic chemical; a salt of phosphoric acid.

Physician's Desk Reference (PDR): A thick volume that provides a guide to all prescription drugs available in the United States as well as the dosage and side effect information.

Psychological: Mental or emotional as opposed to physical in nature.

Postpartum Depression (PPD): A form of severe depression following delivery that requires treatment. It is sometimes said that postpartum depression occurs within four weeks of delivery but it can happen a few days or even months after childbirth.

Postural Hypotension: A drop in blood pressure when standing up too quickly from a lying or sitting position, causing a lightheaded or woozy feeling. Sometimes called a "head-rush." A symptom that could indicate adrenal fatigue syndrome.

Potassium: The most abundant mineral in a cell. Usually people with adrenal fatigue syndrome have too much potassium in relation to sodium.

Pulse: The rhythmic contraction and expansion of an artery due to the surge of blood from the beat of the heart.

Respiratory System: The system for taking in oxygen and emitting carbon dioxide.

Reverse Osmosis: A process by which a solvent such as water is purified of solutes by being forced through a semi permeable membrane through which the solvent, but not the solutes, may pass.

Scientific Mindset: The idea that emotions and feelings have little bearing on health.

Shock: A critical condition brought on by a sudden drop in blood flow through the body.

Sleep Aids: A sedative or hypnotic drug, especially a barbiturate, in the form of a pill or capsule used to relieve insomnia.

Sleep Apnea: Sleep apnea is a condition in which breathing stops for more than 10 seconds during sleep. Sleep apnea is a major, though often unrecognized, cause of daytime sleepiness.

Sleep Deprivation: The condition of being robbed of normal sleep cycles.

Sodium: A mineral responsible for maintaining blood pressure, as well as moderating water levels in cells. Crucial to the treatment of adrenal fatigue syndrome.

Stress: A physical, mental, or emotional factor that causes bodily or mental tension.

Supplementation: The provision of supplementary substances such as enzymes, vitamins, and minerals.

Syndrome: A group of symptoms that collectively indicate or characterize a disease, psychological disorder, or other abnormal condition.

Synthetic Hormones: Artificial chemical formulations that are not identical in structure or chemical composition to the hormones your body produces on its own.

Tendon: A cord or band of inelastic tissue connecting a muscle to its bony attachment.

Toxins: Substances that interfere with or inhibit healthy function of the body.

Undenatured Whey Protein: One of the two major protein groups that account for about 80% of the total protein in bovine milk, while whey proteins account for the remaining 20%. Whey is derived as a natural byproduct of the cheese-making process. At the time of purchase, most commercial whey protein has already begun to oxidize or may even be completely oxidized. In either case, it is considered to be "denatured."

Vitamin: Any of a group of organic substances essential in small quantities to ensure normal metabolism.

LaVergne, TN USA
18 July 2010
189928LV00001B/1/P